Birdwise

FEDERATION OF
Ontario Naturalists

Birdwise

Pamela M. Hickman

Illustrations by Judie Shore

Kids Can Press Ltd.

Toronto

Written by Pamela M. Hickman for The Federation of
Ontario Naturalists

Kids Can Press Ltd. gratefully acknowledges the
assistance of the Canada Council and the Ontario Arts
Council in the production of this book.

The sonogram on page 65 is reproduced courtesy of
the Cornell Laboratory of Ornithology and the
Federation of Ontario Naturalists.

Canadian Cataloguing in Publication Data

Main entry under title:
Birdwise

Includes index.
ISBN 0-921103-66-2 (bound) ISBN 0-921103-58-1
(pbk.)

1. Birds–Juvenile literature.   2. Birds–Identification–
Juvenile literature.   3. Bird watching–Juvenile
literature.   I. Shore, Judie.   II. Federation of
Ontario Naturalists

QL676.2.B57   1988   j598   C88-093892-7

Book design by Michael Solomon
Edited by Valerie Wyatt
Typeset by Compeer Typographic Services Limited
Printed and bound in Canada by John Deyell Company

88 0 9 8 7 6 5 4 3 2 1

CONTENTS

Bird Parts

What happened here? Do the feathers
and talons give you a clue? After you've
guessed, turn to page 96 to see if you
were right. Then read on to find out
how birds' body parts help them
survive.

What's in a name?

When you were born, your parents had to choose your name. You may be named after an older relative, a special friend, a movie star or any number of special people or things. In many cases, the names of birds are also chosen for special reasons.

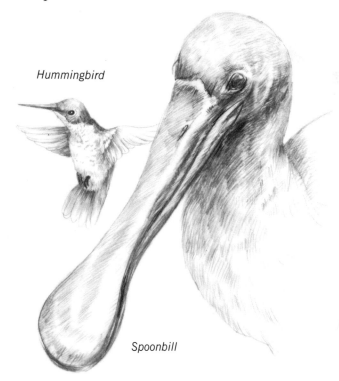

Hummingbird

Spoonbill

Mini-descriptions

The names of some birds are mini-descriptions of what the bird looks like. For example, the Red-tailed Hawk, Scarlet Tanager, Yellow-headed Blackbird and Red-headed Woodpecker are named for their special colouring. It's a little bit like nicknaming a friend Red or Sandy.

Sometimes a bird's distinguishing feature gives it its name. Spoonbills and grosbeaks are examples of birds named for the interesting shape or size of their beaks.

Noisy names

The sound a bird makes has often resulted in its name. The Bobwhite and Whip-poor-will, for instance, are named for their call. The Gray Catbird has a mew-like call, very similar to a real cat. Hummingbirds probably got their name from the humming sound produced by their rapidly beating wings.

People and places

Scientists who discover an animal or plant that has never been seen before sometimes have their find named after them. Names such as Wilson's Warbler, Lincoln's Sparrow, and many others owe their names to the people who first recorded them. Lucy Hunter Baird was lucky enough to have a birdwatching friend name a species after her: Lucy's Warbler.

Habitat is another common reason for a bird's name. The Burrowing Owl, for instance, gets its name from its unusual habit of nesting in burrows in the ground. It's not difficult to guess where the Arctic Tern, Tundra Swan, Boreal Chickadee, Marsh Wren, Pine Warbler or Mountain Bluebird can be found. But beware—there are always exceptions to these general rules. For instance, the Prairie Warbler is *not* found on the prairies!

Burrowing Owl

If you were named for your eating habits, what would your name be?

Edible names

As you might expect, sapsuckers feed on tree sap (and insects), kingfishers eat fish and the Acorn Woodpecker dines on acorns. What do you think oystercatchers, honeysuckers and antwrens eat? The nuthatch gets its name not just from what it eats, but also how it eats. This small bird places seeds and nuts in the grooves of tree bark and then hammers away with its beak until the hard shell cracks, hatching out the tasty bits inside.

Nuthatch

Scientific names

In addition to a common name, like Blue Jay, each bird also has a scientific name in Latin. This helps people all over the world recognize the name of a bird, since common names can differ from country to country. For instance, in North America we are familiar with the Common Loon, but Europeans call the same bird a Black-throated Diver. By using its scientific name, *Gavia immer*, everyone knows what you are talking about.

Here's a picture of an imaginary bird. Using some of the ideas for naming birds, you decide what to call this "newly discovered species." You'll have to imagine what colour it is!

9

Take a peek at a beak

Next time you visit the zoo, take a look at all the different kinds of beaks birds have. Each beak shape is designed for eating a certain type of food—fish, mammals, insects, fruit and nuts, or nectar. By looking at the shape of a bird's beak you can guess at its main food source and sometimes even its habitat (where it lives). Beaks are also important clues to help you identify birds. Try to match these birds' beaks with the food they eat. (Answers on page 96.)

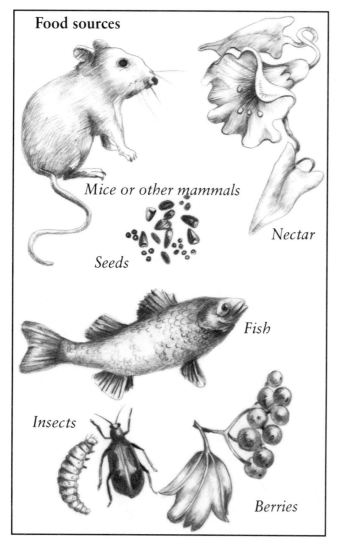

Food sources

Mice or other mammals

Seeds

Nectar

Fish

Insects

Berries

Pelican
My scoop-like beak helps me trap slippery food. What do I eat?

Hummingbird
My straw-like beak is perfect for poking into things and sucking up food. What do I eat?

Swift
My beak may be small and weak but it opens wide like a vacuum cleaner to help me catch food in mid-air. What do I eat?

Waxwing
My short, slightly hooked beak is great for picking things. What do I eat?

Cardinal
My thick, conical beak is terrific for crunching and cracking food. What do I eat?

Hawk
My strong, hooked beak can tear food apart. What do I eat?

11

Feet are neat

Imagine what it would be like if you walked around on your tip-toes all day. That's what birds do. In fact, what we usually call a bird's feet are really just its toes.

Most birds have four toes. Three point forward and one points back. Birds use their feet for lots of different jobs. Some feet help a bird defend itself or carry nest material. Other feet help their owners perch or comb their feathers. And because it isn't considered bad manners to eat with your feet in the bird world, many birds use their feet when feeding. The strength and size of a bird's feet often depend on what it eats and how it catches its food. Take a look at how these feet help their owners dine in the wild.

Slippery dinner
An Osprey has sharp, curved talons for catching fish. Its toes have pads that are hard and rough with bumps on the insides. The bumps help the Osprey to hold onto its slippery prey. Also, the talons lock into place once the pads strike a fish.

Dig it!
The grouse has thick, strong toes for scratching the ground to uncover food. So do partridges and pheasants.

Hold on!
If you're going to cling to a tree while you eat, you need great grabbing feet like this woodpecker. Nuthatches and creepers have similar feet.

Foot to mouth

Parrots are the only birds that can use their feet to bring food up to their mouths. With two toes pointed forward and two pointed backward, a parrot can get a very tight grip on slippery food like nuts, seeds and fruit.

A hand-y foot

Even little chickadees use their feet for eating. While holding a seed against a hard surface with one foot, the chickadee's beak hammers away until the seed cracks open, releasing the good stuff inside.

B-I-G eaters

The size of the talons on a bird of prey depends on the size of its food. The talons of the South American Harpy Eagle are as big as the claws of a grizzly bear. It can grab huge prey, sometimes even small sheep. On the other hand (or should we say "foot"), the Barn Owl, which feeds on small animals like mice, can make do with much smaller feet.

Asleep on their feet?

Ever wonder why birds don't fall out of trees when they sleep? They have special muscles and tendons in their legs that act like built-in locks. When a bird is perching or sleeping, its toes are automatically pulled into a tight "fist" around the branch, keeping the bird from falling.

Hide and seek

Birds would be great at hide and seek. Many of them are coloured so that they blend in with their surroundings. This "camouflage" helps them avoid predators.

One master of camouflage is the American Bittern. Its brown and white striped breast allows it to disappear among the cat-tails and reeds in its marsh home. Instead of flying away when frightened, the bittern simply freezes. Because it stays still and is so well camouflaged, it is very difficult to see.

Camouflage works well both for birds hiding from predators and for hunting birds trying to sneak up on their prey. As their name suggests, Snowy Owls, which live in the Arctic, blend in very well with snow and ice. This helps them surprise lemmings, their main food source.

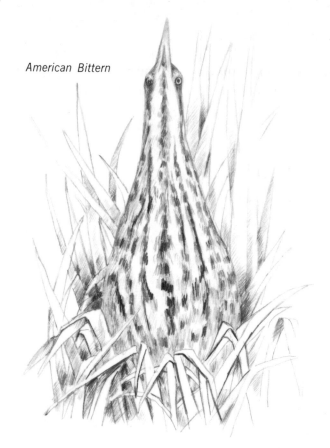

American Bittern

Male and female Red-winged Blackbirds

Mr., Mrs., or Ms?

Usually the female of a species is better camouflaged than the male. For example, the male cardinal is brilliant red, while the female is a dull grey-olive. A male's brilliant plumage helps him attract a mate, but it's not very useful when incubating the eggs or raising the young. For these jobs, birds want to blend in with their surroundings to avoid attracting predators. Usually the dullest coloured parent spends more time sitting on the nest.

Sometimes a brightly coloured male helps his dull-coloured mate with egg-sitting duties. When this happens, you can be sure that their nest is well hidden, so camouflage isn't as important.

Some baby birds, such as Red-winged Blackbirds, Bobolinks and cardinals, are dully coloured like their mothers. This helps them escape the notice of hungry predators.

Covering up

You might expect birds to hide their nests carefully, but many nest out in the open. These nests, however, are usually high up in trees or on cliffs and islands that are hard to reach. Birds that nest near the ground do camouflage their nests. The Least Bittern's nest is built in marshes on a bed of reeds, grasses and wild irises. In order to hide the nest from above, the bittern weaves a roof of reeds.

Least Bittern Nest

Temporary camouflage is important when the parents leave a nest, even for a few minutes. The Ruffed Grouse, for example, carefully covers its nest with leaves before going off to find food. Eider ducks cover their eggs with the down feathers that line the nest. That not only keeps the duckling eggs hidden —it also keeps them warm and protects them from the hot sun.

A perfect match

Eggs can also be camouflaged. Ground nesters such as Killdeer, Common Snipe and Blue Grouse often have buff-coloured eggs that are speckled, blotched or otherwise marked with browns. This colouring helps the eggs blend in with sand and pebbles on a beach or the dead leaves on a woodland floor. Eggs laid in dark holes or burrows, like those of woodpeckers, owls, kingfishers or swifts, have little need to be camouflaged and are snowy white.

Egg camouflage

An Eider duck on her downy nest

15

Binocular eyes

Even without using a pair of binoculars, you have binocular vision—and so do many birds. Binocular vision means that both eyes focus on an object at the same time. To have binocular vision, both eyes must point forward, like yours do. Binocular vision allows you to judge how big an object is and how far away. Owls and other hunting birds depend on their binocular vision when they hunt.

Birds that don't have to hunt to survive don't need binocular vision. Instead, they have monocular vision. Their eyes are located on the sides of their heads and because of this, only one eye at a time can focus on an object. If you've ever watched a robin search for a worm you've seen monocular vision in action. The robin stops every few steps and tilts its head to the side so that one eye can focus on the grass and hidden worms. Monocular vision doesn't allow birds to judge distance or size nearly as well as binocular vision, but it has other advantages. One eye can be looking at food while the other eye is checking in the opposite direction for predators.

Most birds have both monocular *and* binocular vision in varying amounts. The greater their binocular vision, the better their eyesight.

Roving eyes
You can move your eyes up and down and from side to side to see things without turning your head. The eyes of birds, however, are fixed in their sockets and cannot move. To make up for this, birds have very flexible necks. They have an average of fourteen bones in their necks (mammals, like you, have only seven) and can swing their heads around with lightning speed.

Make a binocular poncho

There's nothing worse than being rained on when you're out birdwatching. Your feet get wet, your head gets wet — even your binoculars get wet. This binocular poncho puts an end to wet binoculars.

You'll need: a circular piece of heavy plastic large enough to cover the binoculars when hung around your neck
scissors
binoculars with neck strap

1. Cut two holes in the plastic to match up with the neck strap hooks on your binoculars.

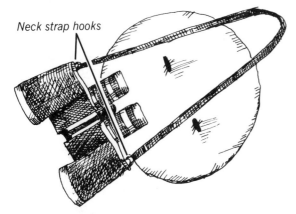

Neck strap hooks

2. Hook the neck straps into the binoculars through the holes.

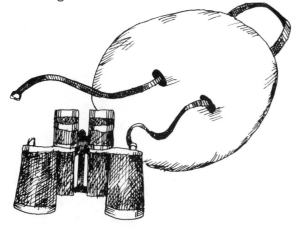

3. The poncho will hang down, covering the binoculars when they are not being used. When you want to use them, simply flip back the poncho.

Birds of a feather

Despite Peter Pan's encouraging words, it takes more than belief to be able to fly. Feathers are a good start, and birds are the only living creatures that have them. A feather may look simple, but it is actually amazingly well designed to help birds fly, keep them warm or cool as needed and help them hide or attract a mate. No other animal growth is as strong, lightweight and flexible as a bird's feather.

Four feathers

There are four different kinds of feathers. *Contour feathers* are the ones covering the bird's body, giving it shape as well as colour. They include the long, stiff flight feathers found in the wings and tail. *Filoplumes* are hair-like feathers growing around the base of the contour feathers. Some birds, such as ducks and geese, have *down feathers* beneath the contour feathers. These are especially important for warmth. Herons and bitterns have *powder-down feathers*, which disintegrate into a powdery substance used by the birds when preening. The powder acts like dry shampoo, cleaning the feathers and keeping them in flying shape. Other birds preen with oil from an oil gland at the base of their tails.

Feathered rainbows

Part of the joy of birdwatching is seeing the gorgeous rainbow of feather colours. What gives feathers their colour? Believe it or not, there's very little colour *in* feathers. Most of the colour you see comes from light bouncing off the feathers. A feather acts like a prism. When light falls on the feather, it breaks apart into a rainbow of colours. Some of these colours are absorbed by the feather, while others are reflected. It is the reflected colour that you see. The breeding plumage of hummingbirds, grackles and starlings is iridescent, changing colour as the bird moves in the light. The result is a shimmering, multi-coloured display that's beautiful to watch. Colour serves two main purposes: to camouflage a bird so that it can avoid hungry predators or to make a bird stand out so that it can attract a mate.

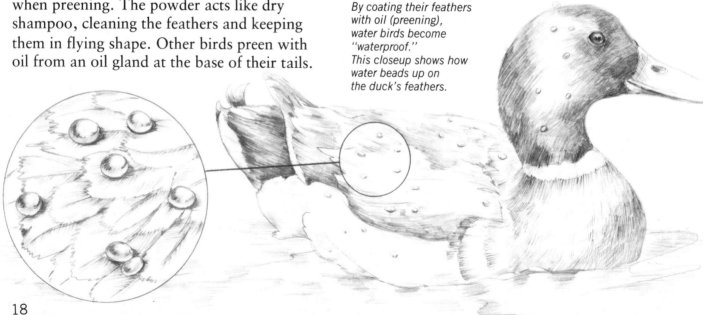

By coating their feathers with oil (preening), water birds become "waterproof." This closeup shows how water beads up on the duck's feathers.

Bald birds?

At least once a year birds replace all their feathers with new ones. This is called moulting. But don't expect to see a bunch of balding birds. Most species only lose one or two feathers at a time so that they can still fly. However, ducks, geese and some other water birds that don't have to fly to catch their food are flightless for a short time while their new flight feathers grow in.

Moulting usually occurs after the nesting season, but a full or partial moult may also take place before breeding. This allows some males to change into their flashy colours. Ptarmigans undergo a *third* moult in the fall, when they turn white to blend in with the snow.

A ptarmigan in summer . . .

and in winter

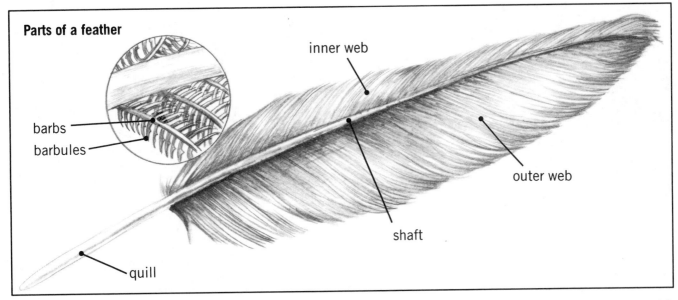

Parts of a feather

barbs

barbules

inner web

outer web

shaft

quill

Start a feather collection

You don't have to pluck a chicken to collect feathers. Birds moult at least once a year, and you can often find their feathers on the ground, especially near their nests. A feather collection can help you compare the feathers of different birds and different feathers of the same bird. You can also look at how the feather is constructed and coloured.

You'll need: feathers
several sheets of three-ring binder paper
glue or tape
a pen
clear plastic food wrap (optional)
a binder

1. Collect feathers and arrange them attractively on sheets of paper. You may wish to organize the feathers by size, colour or type of bird. Glue or tape the feathers to the paper.

2. Label each feather as well as you can. Include species (if known), where it was found (city and habitat) and when.

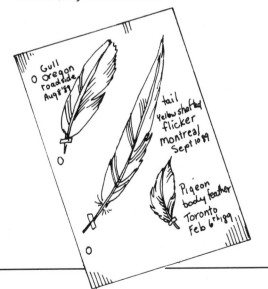

3. You can cover each page with a clear plastic wrapping to protect the feathers. Colours will fade over time.

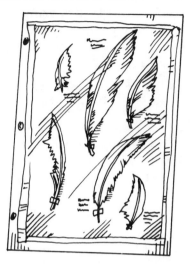

4. Store your collection in a binder.

Up, up and away

Have you ever watched a bird soaring overhead and wished you could join it? Many people have, and some have even invented equipment to help them get airborne. For instance, there's the legend of Icarus, who strapped on bird wings held together with wax. He flew quite well—until he got too near the sun and the wax melted. Early attempts by real-life human flyers didn't fare much better. They leapt off cliffs, castles and tree branches . . . and came crashing down. Flying, it soon became clear, was for the birds. But just exactly how do they do it?

Birds have five basic flying techniques: flapping, gliding, soaring, fluttering and hovering. Most birds use at least two of these; some use all five. Sometimes birds use a combination of flight patterns. Goldfinches, for instance, quickly alternate between flapping and gliding to produce a roller coaster-like flight.

No-flap flyer

Albatrosses can fly for hours over the ocean without flapping their wings. They hold their wings out steadily and glide. The Wandering Albatross has a lot of wing to hold up—its wingspan is as wide as a car is long!

Flying facts

- Canvasback Ducks can fly more than 113 kph (70 mph) when migrating. That's faster than cars travel on the highway.
- Peregrine Falcons have hit twice that speed when diving.
- Bar-headed Geese may be the highest flying birds. They have been sighted flying more than 8.8 km (5$\frac{1}{2}$ miles) up in the air.

Ring-billed Gulls

Turkey Vulture

Hover over

Have you ever watched a gull hover over a boat? It flaps its wings but doesn't seem to move ahead. That's because the wind blowing against the bird keeps it from going forward. The bird hangs in the air in this way so it can quickly swoop down and pick up any food leftovers from the boat.

Hitchhikers

Catching a ride on a rising air current is an effortless way to fly. It leaves your attention free to watch what's happening below. Perhaps that's why hawks and Turkey Vultures soar when they're looking for a meal.

Robin

Kestrel

In a flap

Flapping is the most common way of flying. When a robin or a sparrow wants to get from place to place, that's exactly what it does. Who is the fastest flapper of them all? See "Flying facts" on page 22.

Flutter-fly

By flapping their wings fast, some birds can stay in one place. Hummingbirds are champion flutterers, but kestrels also flutter when catching their food.

How Birds Live

What will happen to the baby bird that hatched out of this shell? Will it learn to fly, migrate south in winter and come back to start a family of its own? Turn the page to see how birds live day to day and season to season.

Nest watching

Nests are like the birds that build them. They come in a variety of sizes and shapes. For example, the largest known bird's nest in North America belonged to a Florida Bald Eagle. It weighed the same as two compact cars and it was bigger than a hot tub. At the other end of the scale is the tiny nest of the Ruby-throated Hummingbird. It's smaller than an egg cup.

What are nests made of? Sticks, mosses, lichens, grasses, mud, feathers, bark, straw and rootlets are popular nest-building materials. But some birds such as hummingbirds, some warblers, bushtits and Blue-gray Gnatcatchers even steal spider silk and use it to reinforce their nests.

A hummingbird nest, actual size

An eagle's nest

Weaverbird nest

Watching a bird build a nest is fascinating. Some birds work with painstaking care; others just slap their nests together. Often it's the female that builds the nest, but sometimes the male will help out. A dramatic example of nest-building skill is found in the weaverbirds of Africa, India and Australia. They actually weave grass into a basket-like nest, just like a person might weave a basket. Could it be that ancient people learned how to make baskets by watching weaverbirds?

Be careful!

You can learn a lot about birds by watching them build a nest and take care of their eggs. One of the first things you must learn is to be careful.

Great care must be taken not to disturb the nest or the young. Parents may be frightened off by too much attention, leaving their young to starve. Some parents become very angry when their nest is approached and will attack an intruder. In some places "BEWARE OF BIRD" signs have to be posted to keep people away from nests and protective parents. Watching from a bird blind is a good way to make sure you don't disturb parents and young. See page 62 for information on how to build one. If you're careful, you can watch a nest over the entire breeding period and see as the young hatch, grow, learn to fly and fledge (leave the nest on their own).

Take note

To help you compare the family life of different species and help you remember some of the details of your hours spent nest-watching, keep a daily journal of your observations describing the activities at the nest. You can make notes on feeding habits, daily routines, changes in appearance of the young and many other interesting features. If you have a camera, some photographs of the nest and young at different stages of development would provide wonderful highlights to your diary.

A year-round hobby

After the breeding season is over, you can look for nests. They are especially easy to spot if you live in an area where the trees lose their leaves in autumn. An abandoned nest can provide you with a chance to get a really close-up view of how the nest is constructed. In addition, you may be able to identify the nest's owners using a field guide to bird nests. Even though they are no longer being used by the owners, these nests should not be removed. Sometimes old nests are used as shelter later in the year by other species. In some cases, nests are reused by their owners for several years, or the abandoned nest of one bird may be taken over by a different bird the following year.

Nests to notice

Here are some neat nests to get you started on a nest-watching hobby.

A make-do nest
The Cliff Swallow builds an unusual gourd-shaped nest with a narrow side entrance leading to an enlarged chamber. If no cliff is available, the nest is tucked under the eaves of a barn or other building. In a barn, local materials are used— straw, mud and even horsehair!

Nest, sweet nest
The Osprey builds a large cup-shaped nest of sticks, twigs, driftwood and weed stalks and lines it with grass, algae or feathers. Although they are usually built in a treetop near water, Osprey nests are also found on buildings and hydro poles. The Osprey often uses the same nest year after year, renovating and enlarging it each year.

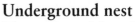

Underground nest
The male and female Belted Kingfishers deserve a medal for nest engineering. They dig a burrow as long as a canoe paddle in a steep river or pond bank and lay their eggs on the bare floor of a circular chamber at the end of the burrow. As feeding occurs, fish bones pile up on the floor, providing the young with a prickly mattress.

Secret entrance

The Marsh Wren weaves grasses and reed stalks into a ball-shaped nest and lines it with finer grasses, cat-tail down and feathers. Found in cat-tail marshes, these small nests have a clever side entrance that helps to hide the eggs and young from predators flying overhead. Although the eggs are laid in only one nest, male Marsh Wrens build several nests to fool their enemies.

Tree nest

The Hairy Woodpecker drills a gourd-shaped nesting cavity into live trees, sometimes in maple swamps or apple orchards. It doesn't bother to build a nest in the cavity; it just lines the hole with wood chips.

29

To nest or not to nest . . .

Some birds, such as Nighthawks and Whip-poor-wills, don't build nests at all. They lay their eggs directly on the ground. Marsh Wrens, on the other hand, often build three or four nests among the cat-tails in their breeding territory to outsmart predators.

The cowbird is even sneakier — or should we say lazier? It doesn't build a nest. Instead, it lays individual eggs in the nests of other birds. When the young cowbird hatches, it is raised by foster parents, often taking food from the bird's other young. Yellow Warblers have a simple but effective way of dealing with unwelcome cowbird eggs. They simply cover up the unwanted egg with new nesting material, creating a second floor in the nest. With the intruder-egg out of the way, it's business as usual.

Can you spot the foster baby? See page 96.

A roof overhead

The Ovenbird digs a hole in the ground and weaves together a nest of grasses, dry leaves and bark strips lined with hair, fine grasses or pine needles. Overhead it builds an arch of leaves and grass, leaving an entrance at one side.

A hanging nest

Weave together a nest out of plant fibres, string, bark, yarn, grasses and hair and hang it from the tip of a branch (in large trees) or near the trunk (in small trees) and you've got a nest a Northern Oriole would feel at home in.

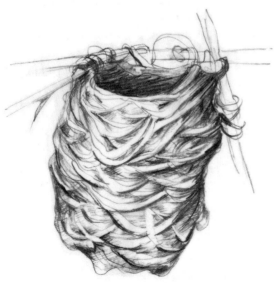

Sack nest

The Common Bushtit may be small, but its nest isn't. Its hanging, sack-like nest may be as long as a loaf of bread. Spider webs are used to hold together the oak catkins, dried leaves, mosses and lichens it's made of.

Affordable housing

With a few simple materials you can become an architect for birds. By building one of these birdhouses you can attract a feathered family to your yard and watch the amazing transformation from egg to independent young.

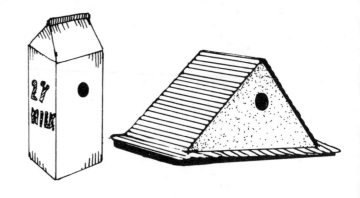

Milk carton birdhouse

Milk cartons are great for holding more than just milk. You can turn one into a "bird carton."

You'll need: a 2-L (or 2-quart) waxed cardboard milk carton
scissors
50 cm (20 inches) of strong but bendable wire
2 nails
a hammer
waterproof packing tape
dried grasses

1. Open up the top of the carton and wash it out well with warm water and a brush.
2. Cut out a circle 4 cm (1½ inches) in diameter on one side of the container, about 5 cm (2 inches) below the bend in the carton.

3. On the opposite side of the carton, poke two holes with a nail. The top hole should be one-third of the way down from the bend and the second hole about two-thirds of the way down.

4. Thread the wire into the top hole, down the carton on the inside, and out of the bottom hole.

5. Place a little bit of dried grasses in the bottom of the carton.
6. Seal the top of the carton back up with waterproof packing tape.
7. To put your birdhouse up, choose a pole or tree in an open area. Hammer your nails into the tree so that they are spaced about 30 cm (12 inches) apart, one above the other.

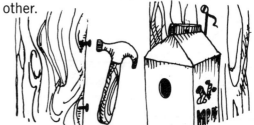

8. Wrap one end of the wire around each nail so that the birdhouse is firmly attached to the tree.

Popsicle stick birdhouse

After you've slurped away your popsicle on a hot summer day, save the stick for a winter birdhouse building project. This easy-to-build house will attract nearby House Wrens.

You'll need: 72 popsicle sticks
a 35 × 23 cm (14 × 9 inches) piece of cork, 10 mm (¼ inch) thick
a 26 × 10 cm (10¼ × 4 inches) piece of cork, 10 mm (¼ inch) thick
a sharp knife
white glue
a 26 × 10 cm (10¼ × 4 inches) piece of plywood, 10 mm (¼ inch) thick
3-4 nails
a hammer

1. Ask an adult to cut the cork, using a sharp knife. From the 35 × 23 cm (14 × 9 inches) piece, cut two triangles with all sides measuring 23 cm (9 inches).
2. In one cork triangle only, cut a hole 2.5 cm (1 inch) in diameter in the centre.

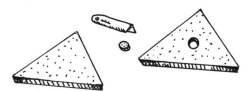

3. On your 26 × 10 cm (10¼ × 4 inches) piece of cork, glue 26 popsicle sticks side by side, across the 26 cm (10¼ inch) side, so they are touching. This will form the floor of your birdhouse.

4. Glue your cork triangle with the hole, upright, on to the floor, about 12 mm (½ inch) from the front edge (long edge) and from each side.
5. Glue the solid cork triangle about 12 mm (½ inch) from the back edge.

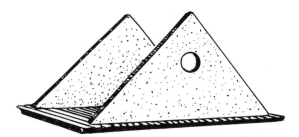

6. Glue 23 popsicle sticks, side by side, on each side of the birdhouse so that they are attached to both front and back pieces of cork.
7. When you get to the peak, two sticks will meet. Put a bead of glue along the whole length of this join.

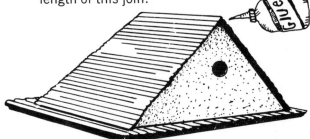

8. Set your plywood on a tree branch or pole near shrubs, about 2 m (6 feet) above the ground. Hammer the nails into the pole or tree to secure the wood.
9. Glue the bottom of your birdhouse to this wooden platform.

Family life

If you are lucky enough to have a family living in your birdhouse, you'll be able to learn a great deal about what happens during the breeding season. Some activities, however, go on behind closed doors. Here's what you would see if you could shrink down to egg-size and spend some time in the nest.

Egg-zamining eggs

After the nest is finished, egg laying begins. Perching birds, such as sparrows or wrens, usually lay one egg per day, often early in the morning. Gulls, hawks and owls lay every other day. Different species lay different numbers of eggs in a year. If you're visiting a pheasant nest, be prepared for a crowd! A pheasant may lay 12 to 15 eggs in one clutch. An albatross, on the other hand, lays just one egg. There are two types of egg layers: determinate and indeterminate. A determinate layer will produce a specified number of eggs and then stop, regardless of what happens to the eggs. An indeterminate layer will keep on laying eggs, replacing damaged or stolen ones, until a certain clutch size is reached.

Not all eggs are egg-shaped. Owl eggs are nearly round, while the eggs of murres and other auks are pear-shaped so they don't roll off the narrow cliff ledges on which they are laid. The range of colours found in bird eggs is similar to the range of colours you may get in a bruise. This is because the colours come from by-products of blood and bile.

Egg warmers

For eggs to hatch, they must be kept warm. This "incubation" period can last from 11 to 80 days, depending on the species.

Some birds, such as ducks and grouse, start incubation after all their eggs are laid. In this way, all of the eggs get off to the same start. Large birds, such as owls, storks and herons, however, start to incubate as soon as the first egg appears. This is their way of "family planning." When there is lots of food available, all the chicks may survive, but if it's scarce, nestlings will compete for food. Usually the chicks that hatch first will win out.

Keeping the eggs warm is a major chore. Many adult birds have a "brood patch" on their underbodies. This is a bare patch of skin with lots of blood vessels carrying warm blood. Birds without brood patches provide warmth in other ways. You probably wouldn't want to be incubated by a gannet. It simply puts its large webbed feet over the egg for warmth. And ducks, for example, pull out down feathers and add them to the nest, like a duvet. Wouldn't it be nice to snuggle "down" in that!

Breaking out

Unhatched birds, or "embryos," have a small bump on the tip of their upper beak, called an egg tooth. This is used for chipping away at the egg shell so that they can hatch. Breaking out may take several hours or days. Egg-bound chicks often peep as they work. All that chirping and peeping makes the nest a noisy place. Parents may eat the discarded shell or remove it from the nest.

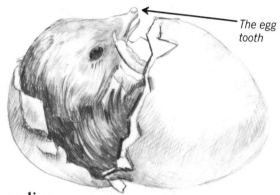

The egg tooth

Brooding

Some young birds, like geese or pheasants, can walk and feed almost immediately. They are called precocial. Others, such as songbirds, are born helpless, blind and naked and are called altricial. After hatching, altricial birds must be kept warm until they grow down feathers. Common Eiders keep their chicks warm, or "brood," for two to seven hours, while Cliff Swallows brood for 21 days. Imagine being squashed together with a bunch of squirming, hungry chicks for three whole weeks!

Soup's on!

Even watching adult birds feed their young can be exhausting. The parent birds make several hundred trips out to find food and back to the nest every day! If you dropped in for a meal, the menu would depend on the species you were visiting. Most young perching birds feed on insects deposited straight into their gaping mouths. Many adult seabirds fill up on food out at sea, semi-digest it and then regurgitate it for the young. A young pelican sticks its whole head into its parent's mouth to get at the goodies. Adult petrels often go for days collecting food at sea. The food is then digested and concentrated into a protein-rich, thick oil that's bright orange. You might not find it appetizing but petrel nestlings love it.

Leaving home

The age at which birds leave the nest, or "fledge," depends on the species. A young warbler may leave its nest after only nine days. Its parents continue to feed it for two more weeks. Young Mute Swans, however, stay with their parents for nine months, even though they can swim and feed on their own soon after hatching.

These two birds have just hatched. One is precocial, the other is altricial. Can you tell which is which?

On the move

How do birds find their way from summer breeding grounds to winter feeding areas? Why do they migrate? Unfortunately, birds can't talk, so we can't know for certain their answers to these questions. But we can ask an ornithologist (a scientist who studies birds). Here Dr. Ian Kirkham answers some of the most often asked questions about migration.

Q. What is migration?

A. Migration is the seasonal movement of birds and other animals. There are three types of migration: diurnal, nocturnal and altitudinal. Diurnal migration takes place during the day (diurnal means day). Birds that fly at night are called nocturnal migrants (nocturnal means night). Unlike diurnal and nocturnal migration, altitudinal migration may take only a few minutes. In the fall, birds nesting high up in the mountains fly down to lower slopes or valleys where winter conditions are better. In the spring, the birds return to the higher altitudes. Instead of flying thousands of kilometres to reach a suitable habitat, altitudinal migrants can get there much faster and easier—a bit like taking an elevator!

Q. Why do birds migrate?

A. There may be several reasons for migration. It may be triggered by reduced hours of sunlight or by a shortage of food. Or maybe cold temperatures start birds migrating or, in the spring, the instinct to return to breeding grounds. But not all birds pay attention to these signs, since not all species migrate.

Q. How do birds find their way?

A. Some birds, such as young geese, follow their parents during migration, but the young of many other species have to find their own way south. How they do it has puzzled scientists for a long time. Some birds may follow mountain ranges and coastlines, like a map. Others, however, migrate across oceans where no landmarks are found. One theory is that migrating birds use the stars or angle of the sun to help find their way, like pilots and sailors do. Although there are still some mysteries about migration, one thing is certain; birds not only get where they're going, but also get there at almost the same time every year.

Q. How far do birds travel when they migrate?

A. It depends on the bird. Lots of North American birds travel to Central or South America and back, a distance of as much as 3000 kilometres (1800 miles). But some amazing migrants travel even farther. The Arctic Tern, for example, flies from the far North to the southern tip of South America and the edge of Antarctica's pack ice. Its round-trip migration is farther than the distance around the earth, making it the longest migration of any animal.

Migration marvels

▫ *Whooping Cranes come every year to lay their eggs in the Aransas National Wildlife Reserve in southern Texas. Because the cranes always return to the same place, scientists can count exactly how many there are from year to year.*

▫ *In San Juan Capistrano, California, people almost set their watches by the massive return of the swallows. It happens every year on March 19.*

▫ *In Pembroke, Ontario, an annual Festival of Swallows is celebrated in August. Nearly 200 000 swallows invade the town on a migration stopover.*

Believe it or not

In ancient times, people had strange ideas about the seasonal appearance and disappearance of some birds.

▫ *Aristotle, the ancient Greek philosopher, believed that birds didn't go anywhere, but simply changed their identity with another species. For instance, he said that as summer approached, the European Robin became a European Redstart. This explained why the redstart appeared and the robin disappeared.*

▫ *Some naturalists thought that only large birds could migrate across oceans. They believed that smaller birds hitchhiked on the backs of others.*

▫ *In 1703, an Englishman wrote that birds flew to the moon over a period of 60 days and then went into hibernation.*

Birdfeeder checklist

You can keep track of the birds that live in your area or pass through during migration by making a bird checklist. It will help you remember which birds you saw and allow you to compare the number and kinds of birds from year to year. Scientists also keep these types of records to find out whether bird populations are going up or down and whether birds are moving into new areas.

A nearby birdfeeder is a good place to start your checklist. If the food is good, it's bound to attract lots of birds.

You'll need: a pad of paper
a pen or pencil
a field guide to birds
binoculars (if you have them)

1. Set up your paper in columns with these headings across the top: Species, No. of individuals, Date, Time, Weather, Remarks.

2. Choose the best spot in your house for watching your feeder and leave your chart and a pencil on a table nearby. Ask anyone who sees a bird at the feeder to fill in the chart.

3. At the end of the feeding season make a list of the different species of birds that visited your feeder. This list can be compared with those of past and future years. Use the other information to figure out the most popular time of day and best weather for feeding.

4. The same checklist can be used when you're birdwatching in the field. Carry a small pad of paper or use index cards for recording your findings.

Counting on birds

There are lots of birds out there to count. About 645 species of birds live in North America, north of Mexico. Some keen birdwatchers, who keep a list of all the different species they have ever seen (called a Life List), have spotted 500 or more species. Even an amateur can hope to see 300.

In some areas there are Birder Hotlines. Phone into one of these hotlines and you'll hear what new rare birds have been seen in the area.

Word travels like wildfire, and soon all the local birdwatchers are on the lookout.

To get started on your bird counting career, you might want to help out during a local bird count. These are official days established by naturalists' groups to count birds in an area. And they can always use an extra pair of eyes. Contact your local naturalists' group for more information.

Warming up in winter

The American Goldfinch in winter and in summer (circle)

If you live in a climate where the winters are cold and snowy, you know that trying to keep warm is a major pastime. Like people, birds have also developed different ways to keep from freezing. In fact, we have learned some of our winter survival tricks from birds!

Feeling down

Many people wear down jackets or vests in the winter for warmth. Down feathers—the soft feathers found on many newly hatched birds and the undercoats of ducks and geese—are great for warmth. Air is trapped between the feathers, acting as an insulator to keep your body heat in and cold air out. Birds also fluff up their natural covering of feathers to trap air and keep warm. Some species can puff up to almost three times their normal size.

Bundle up!

When the winter winds blow, it's time to pull on an extra sweater—and maybe even long underwear. Birds don't have clothes but they *do* grow more feathers for winter warmth. The American Goldfinch, for example, has about a thousand more feathers in winter than in summer.

Snuggle up

Huddling together is a great way of fighting the cold. Chickadees gather in small groups in tree holes to pool body heat. As many as a million starlings may roost together on rooftops, building ledges, in evergreens or other sheltered areas. Why these gigantic slumber parties? Some experts believe that the combined body heat and mass of the birds helps them stay warm and reduces the effect of wind chill.

A nice cold bed

You've heard of the expression "blanket of snow." Well, the Ruffed Grouse takes it seriously. On cold nights, it may dive into a bank or drift of deep, fluffy snow to sleep. The air spaces in the snow provide excellent insulation and the snow itself acts as a perfect camouflage. Smaller birds, such as American Tree Sparrows, Common Redpolls and Snow Buntings, also take shelter under snow in very cold weather. If you think a bed of snow is for the birds, think again. The Inuit in the far North sleep in snow homes, and people stranded because of plane crashes often survive by curling up in a snow bed.

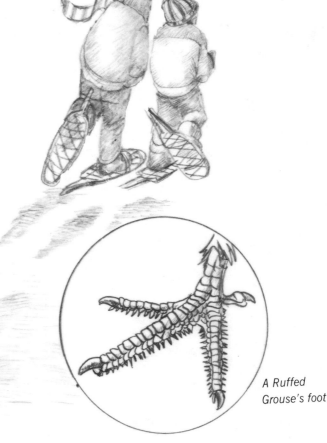

A Ruffed Grouse's foot

Feathered snowshoes

To get around in deep snow, some people wear snowshoes. The snowshoe spreads your weight over a larger surface area and allows you to walk on top of the snow, rather than through it. Some birds grow their own miniature snowshoes in winter. Scaly growths along the toes of Ruffed Grouse help the birds travel easily over the powdery woodland snow. Similarly, ptarmigans grow extra feathers between their toes to help them walk on top of the snow.

41

Some Birds Up Close

Whose feet are these? Here's a hint: there's a hummingbird, a gull, a woodpecker and an owl. Try to figure out which is which and turn to page 96 for the answer. You'll find out more about these birds in this chapter.

Give a hoot!

Few night sounds will tingle your spine like the hoots or shrieks of a nearby owl. Owls are often thought of as mysterious, secretive birds. Perhaps this is because most species of owls are active only at night and people rarely see them. And so we are a bit spooked by them.

Owls are found around the world, but no matter where they live, they share some owlish features. Let's take a look at this Great Horned Owl to see what these features are and why an owl has them.

The better to sneak up on you with

Once an owl has seen or heard its prey, it must move in silently and swiftly. The flight feathers at the edge of its wings have a soft, jagged, comb-like edge, which allows them to whisper through the air. And because an owl's body is light in relation to the size of its wings, it doesn't need to flap as much as other birds, so it makes less noise.

The better to grab you with

When an owl strikes its prey, it stretches out its four toes. The long, sharp talons pierce the vital organs or blood vessels of its prey and death is quick. If the prey is large, the owl will use its talons to carry its prey back to the nest or perch. For smaller prey, the owl uses its beak. The feet are also specially designed so that the outer toe can move forward or backward to give the best grip.

The better to hear you with

Did you ever wonder where an owl's ears are? They are the large slits located on opposite sides of its face feathers. Notice how these face feathers look like a bowl? They funnel sounds into the ears. Since some owls are active only at night, they depend on their hearing to help them find food. Barn Owls and Long-eared Owls rely totally on their exceptional hearing when hunting.

The better to see you with

An owl's eyes are adapted to two very special tasks: seeing in the dark and picking out details from great distances. Both of these abilities are important to a night hunter who, while flying overhead, must spot tiny creatures such as mice. In dim light, an owl can see from 10 to 100 times better than a person. The large size of its eyes and specially shaped eyeballs help it see well. So does its binocular vision—its ability to see its prey with both eyes at the same time. (For more about binocular vision, see page 16.) An owl's eyes cannot rotate up, down or sideways as yours can. To make up for this, an owl can turn its head almost all the way around.

The better to eat you with!

The owl's sharply curved beak is perfect for tearing apart prey. Although it looks like a ferocious weapon, the beak is never used in a fight. The talons are used instead.

Owl prowl

Many species of owls are "nocturnal," or active at night, so the best time to prowl for owls is after dusk.

- Choose your spot carefully. Do some research to find out what kind of habitat various owls prefer. If you've seen an owl before, go back to that spot: you might get lucky again.
- Choose your time. Spring is a good time for your outing because owls are nesting and actively defending their territories.
- Try luring an owl into view by pretending to be a rival. Imitate an owl's call or play a tape recording of a real owl. It may take several tries at different times and locations to get a response.
- Be patient and don't talk or rustle around. If you see an owl, the wait will have been worthwhile.

Owl pellets: nature's jigsaw puzzles

You wouldn't eat a chicken whole, bones and all. You'd spit out the bones and just eat the soft parts. Owls aren't so fussy. They gobble down small mice and voles whole in one gulp, but they can't digest the tough bits. Instead they spit them up in the form of pellets. By dissecting these little "packages" of bones, claws, beaks, teeth, fur and feathers, you can find clues about what an owl has been eating. Scientists use owl pellets to help figure out how owl diets change in different places and seasons and to guess at an owl's role in the local food chain.

Dissecting owl pellets

You don't need to be an expert to dissect an owl's pellet and try to figure out what the bird has been eating. Here's how to do it.

You'll need: owl pellets
Ziplock plastic bags
a dish of warm water
paper towels
tweezers or two skewers
field guides to mammals and
insects

1. Look for owl pellets at the foot of owls' daytime roosts and nests or under nighttime feeding perches.
2. Store them in a Ziplock plastic bag until you're ready to dissect them.

3. Small pellets can be dissected dry, but larger samples should be soaked for an hour or so in a dish of warm water.

4. Put the softened pellets on paper towels. Gently separate the hard parts (bones, teeth, etc.) from the soft parts (fur, feathers, etc.) using the tweezers or skewers.

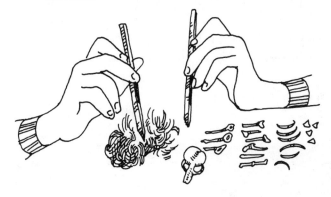

5. Use a field guide to help you identify the different parts. Your most important clues will be the shape, size and teeth pattern of the skulls and the head parts, wings and legs of the insects.

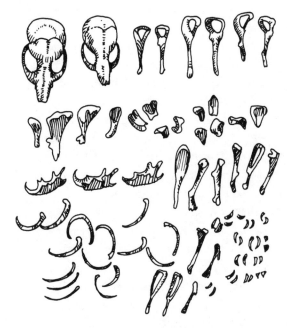

Bones you might find in an owl pellet

47

Gull gossip

Did you know that there is no such bird as a seagull? All gulls have individual names such as California Gull or Bonaparte's Gull. The famous story of Jonathan Livingston Seagull was probably based on a Herring Gull.

Some people think of gulls as pests. But a closer look shows that they're superb examples of birds that are well adapted to life in the wild as well as in the big city.

Like other water birds, gulls spend a lot of time preening their feathers. Preening spreads an oily liquid from a gland at the base of the bird's tail all over the feathers. This makes the feathers waterproof and helps keep them in place.

City slickers

Many gulls have learned to live around people. The Ring-billed Gull is a real city slicker. It'll eat just about anything — french fries, picnic leftovers, garbage — and will nest just about anywhere. You can spot a Ring-billed Gull by the black ring around its yellow bill — and by its screaming and squawking, usually for food. Look for it near open-air restaurants, picnic sites, anywhere there's food. Because the Ring-billed Gull is so at home with people, its numbers have increased dramatically in some areas. In 1973, for example, there were only 400 Ring-billed Gulls nesting in an area of Toronto. Ten years later there were 160 000!

48

Gulls' long, thin wings are great for gliding over land or water. The gulls use updrafts and air currents to keep them airborne.

Helping science

Herring Gulls are used to help find the levels of toxic pollution in the Great Lakes. Scientists monitor the levels of pollutants in the gull eggs. They have found that some egg shells are thinner than normal because of pesticides eaten by the adults. Toxic pollutants have also caused deformities in Herring Gull chicks and unusual behaviour in adults. Over time, experts have found that male Herring Gulls have been more affected by toxic pollution than females have. This is because the pollutants build up in the male gull's body. The female, however, can get rid of some of her body's pollutants when she lays eggs.

Since some gulls live along the ocean, they must be able to drink salt water. Salt is taken out of the bird's blood and passed through a pair of salt glands, each containing, thousands of salt-extracting cells. From here, the salt leaves the body through the bird's nostrils.

Webbed feet act like built-in flippers on water and also give gulls stability on land.

Make a gull-go-round

Follow these simple instructions and create a gull-go-round to hang in your room.

You'll need: tracing paper
a pencil
glue
white bristol board
scissors
magic markers
a field guide to birds
string: 4 pieces 15 cm (6 inches) long and 4 pieces 25 cm (10 inches) long
a dinner plate
a thumb tack

1. Trace the outline of this gull onto tracing paper.
2. Glue the traced gull onto a piece of bristol board and cut out the gull shape. You now have a pattern with which to draw your gulls.
3. Place the gull pattern on the bristol board and trace the outline. Do this eight times to make eight gulls.

4. Cut out your gulls and colour each one as a different species, using a field guide for reference.

5. Use the sharp end of your scissors to punch a small hole in the top wing of each gull. Thread one piece of string through each hole, securing it with a knot. You will end up with four gulls on long strings and four gulls on short strings.

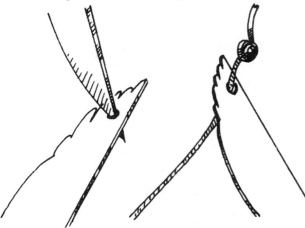

6. To make the disk from which to hang the gulls, trace the outline of a dinner plate on a piece of bristol board. Cut out the dinner-plate-sized circle.

7. Using the pointed end of your scissors, make eight evenly spaced holes along the outer edge of the disk. Make a final hole in the middle.

8. Tie the string from each gull through one of the outer holes, alternating long and short strings.

9. Use a thumb tack to suspend your gull-go-round from the ceiling.

The red spot

Draw a red spot on the bottom half of some of your gulls' beaks. Some species, such as the Herring Gull, have this red spot. When a chick is hungry, it pecks at the spot, which signals the adult to regurgitate food for its young. Imagine if you could just press a button on the refrigerator and get fed!

A *humdinger* of a hummingbird feeder

How much do you drink in a day? Hummingbirds drink seven times their body weight each day. If you drank seven times *your* weight, you'd gulp down more than a hundred cans of pop a day! Because hummingbirds are so thirsty and so beautiful, many people make special feeders to attract them. This hummingbird feeder is easy to make and sure to be a hit.

You'll need: a clean baby food jar with lid
a hammer
a large nail
red enamel paint
a small paintbrush
100 cm (40 inch) piece of thin, bendable wire
125 mL (½ cup) white sugar
600 mL (2½ cups) boiling water
red food colouring
a hook

1. Hammer the nail into the centre of the lid to make a hole about 3 mm (⅛ inch) across. Remove the nail.

2. Turn the lid over and hammer down the sharp edges around the hole.

3. Paint a pretty red flower around the hole on the top of the lid.

4. Fold the wire in two and wrap it around the neck of the jar twice. Twist the ends together to keep the wire around the jar neck.

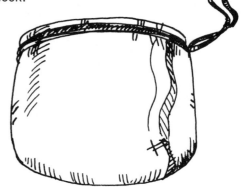

5. Stir the sugar into the water to make your nectar. Do not substitute honey for the sugar. Add a few drops of red food colouring. Let the mixture cool.

6. Pour the nectar into the jar and put the lid on. Put any leftover nectar in the fridge.

7. Twist the tail ends of the wire together and hang your feeder from a hook or nail on your verandah, eaves, or balcony or from a wooden support in your garden.

Your feeder needs to be washed out every week with a little vinegar and a scrub brush. Rinse with water and refill with fresh nectar. If a lot of insects feed on the nectar, rub a little vegetable oil around the opening of the feeder. It will help keep insects, but not hummingbirds, away.

Hovering hummingbirds

How many times can you flap your arms in one second? Chances are you don't even come close to 75. That's how often a hummingbird flaps its wings in just one second. To make this possible, a hummingbird has huge chest muscles that give power to its wings. These flapping muscles make up one-third of the hummingbird's weight.

Hummingbirds are like tiny acrobats. They can fly up, down, backward, forward, sideways and even upside down. Because they hover in front of flowers or feeders, they are easy to watch — until they zip off to the next treat. As you watch a hummingbird fly by, you may hear the distinctive hum of its wings that gives it its name. The humming sound is caused by the vibration of the long primary feathers on the wings.

Hummingbirds eat mainly flower nectar and some insects, so hummingbirds from cold climates must migrate in winter when food becomes scarce. Even though they are among the smallest birds in the world, some hummingbirds fly a long way. The Rufous Hummingbird, for example, migrates between Alaska and Central America. That's a round trip of 8000 km (5000 miles) for a bird no bigger than your thumb!

Woodpecker wonders

You'd probably get a headache if you banged your head against a tree, but woodpeckers don't seem to mind. Their thick head bones act as shock absorbers while extra strong muscles in their head and neck help them work away at a tree for hours. That's not the only amazing thing about woodpeckers. Read on . . . .

Stick out your tongue
Everyone notices the woodpecker's large, strong beak, but have you ever wondered about its tongue? Woodpeckers that eat insects have a tongue like a fishing lure. Barbed hooks along the sides hook into the insect and glue-like saliva finishes the job.

The tongue is attached to bones and elastic-like tissue stored in the woodpecker's head. When the tongue is needed to get at insects inside a tree hole, the whole system slides forward and the tongue shoots out. Fully extended, a woodpecker's tongue can reach up to five times farther than its beak!

Hanging on
How would you like to eat dinner while hanging from the trunk of a tree? Sound tricky? Not for a woodpecker. It has special "hanging on" gear. And best of all, its gear is built in.

The woodpecker has two toes pointed forward and two backward. The back toes, plus its sharp, curved claws, give it a good grip. For extra safety, it props itself up with its tail, which is made of extra stiff feathers.

What's that noise?
Woodpeckers usually tap on trees, but you may get one tapping on your drainpipe or tin roof. Why? Like little children, woodpeckers love to make noise. Since most woodpecker species don't sing like other birds, they tap in order to claim their breeding territory. The noisier the tapping the better the woodpecker likes it, and your drainpipe is a lot louder than a tree. Don't worry though—when it comes to feeding or chiselling out a nesting cavity, these birds stick to trees.

A hole hunt

Put on your detective hat and grab your binoculars. The woodpecker hole hunt is about to begin. Different woodpeckers make different sizes of feeding and nesting holes, as well as different hole patterns. Using their holes as clues, you can identify some of the species living in your area without even seeing them.

One woodpecker, the Yellow-bellied Sapsucker, drills several rows of small holes in live trees in woods and orchards. It feeds on the sap and small insects that collect in the holes.

The large Pileated Woodpecker can make holes big enough to put your whole fist in.

The Acorn Woodpecker, also called the California Woodpecker, stores acorns by drilling holes in tree trunks or poles and then stuffing in one acorn per hole. That's take-out food with a difference!

Watching (and Listening to) Birds

Whoops! These two birds didn't want to
see each other—or be seen. You can
sneak up on birds and even capture
them on film or tape or in your
sketchbook by using some of the tips in
this chapter.

Beginner birdwatching

If you were asked to describe yourself, you might say, "Short, brown hair, blue eyes, freckles, skinny with big feet." This physical description would help a stranger identify you. Birdwatchers also use physical descriptions to help them identify birds.

Name dropping

You may like the idea of being able to see a bird and know its name. The more you birdwatch, the more names you will learn and remember. However, knowing a bird's name is not the most important thing in birdwatching. There are many other ways to identify a bird— by the type of habitat it lives in, what it eats, how it looks or what it is doing. For example, if you can see a bird and recognize it as an insect-eater because it has a narrow, pointed beak, then you are well on your way to becoming a birdwatcher.

When you see a bird . . .

□ Try to estimate the **size** of the bird. Is it closest in size to a sparrow, a robin or a crow?

Robin

Crow

Sparrow

□ Describe the bird's body **shape.** Is it plump like a robin or slender?

Mockingbird

Robin

□ Sometimes different **body parts** stand out as easy identification features. Ask yourself the following questions:
—Does the bird have a crest on its head?
—Are its legs long or short?
—Is its tail forked, squared, pointed or cocked up?

Pigeon

House Wren

Barn Swallow

—Does it have a thick beak, a small, pointed beak or a very long, dagger-shaped beak?

Great Blue Heron

Grosbeak

Warbler

Some birds have **special colouring or markings** that make them easier to remember. Look for eye stripes, speckled or streaked breasts, wingbars, tail stripes and patches of colour.

Hooded Warbler

Western Meadowlark

American Goldfinch

How a bird **moves** can be an important clue to its identity. For instance, the roller-coaster flight of the American Goldfinch helps you identify it at a distance. Take note of where the bird is and what it is doing.
—In the water, is it wading or diving?
—In the air, is it flying straight or up and down? Is it swooping, circling, gliding or hovering?
—On the ground, is it hopping, walking or bobbing?
—On a tree, is it hopping up the bark, climbing down headfirst or climbing up in a spiral pattern?

The bird's **location** can help you identify it. For instance, you're not likely to find a Mallard Duck in a forest or a Great Blue Heron in a dry meadow. They're more likely to be found by a lake. In addition to habitat, the country, state or province where you see a bird is important. All birds have a particular range where you can expect to see them. Some birds have a huge range covering most of North America, while others may be found in certain areas. If you think you have identified a specific bird, check a range map in a field guide just to make sure it actually lives there.

Eastern Meadowlark and range

Look around

You can hear it, but you can't see it. Sound familiar? Some birds are so well hidden that it may take a lot of patience and persistence on your part to find them. Don't forget to look at tree branches, tree trunks, tree tops, fallen logs, rocks, the ground, flower or grass stalks in a field or garden, shoreline or marsh vegetation and hedgerows. Try "spishing." This is a noise you can make, almost like whispering to a friend (*psst*), which can encourage a bird to come out into the open.

When birdwatching, visit as many different habitats as possible, such as a meadow, wood, marsh, lake, ocean, cliff, desert or beach.

Psssssst

60

Dressing for birdwatching

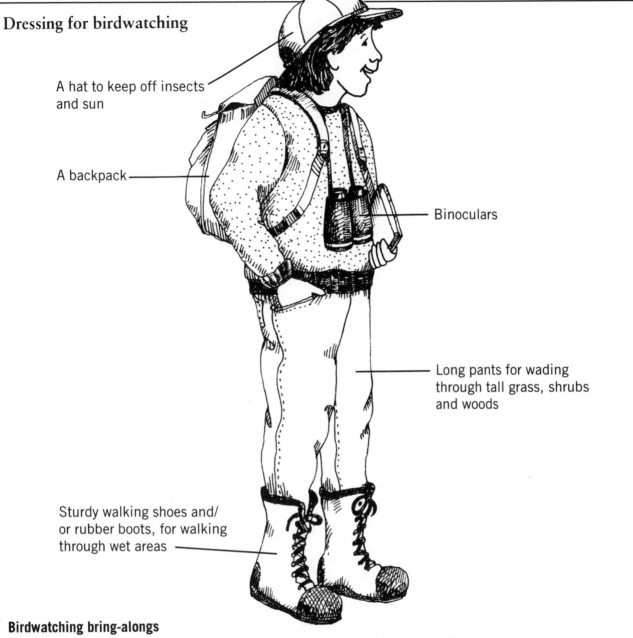

A hat to keep off insects and sun

A backpack

Binoculars

Long pants for wading through tall grass, shrubs and woods

Sturdy walking shoes and/ or rubber boots, for walking through wet areas

Birdwatching bring-alongs

You don't need much, but these items can help make your birdwatching more successful.

- *lunch or snacks for you*
- *a snack for the birds. Chickadees, for example, can be encouraged to feed out of your hand.*
- *a field guide to birds*
- *a bird checklist (many provinces, states and parks have these for visitors)*
- *a pencil*
- *insect repellent (depending on time of year)*

How not to be seen

The most successful birdwatchers are the quietest and best-hidden ones. Like other animals, birds are easily frightened, especially during breeding season. The best way to avoid problems and get the best seat in the house is to make yourself invisible—or close to it! Building a bird blind and dressing to disappear are two good ways to hide from birds.

Seeing blinds

Bird blinds are small enclosures that hide you from the animal you are watching. A photographer will often use a blind to take pictures of wildlife in their natural habitat without scaring them away. There are many different kinds of blinds: some are built on land, others float on water and still others are built up in trees. They may be constructed from natural materials, such as a thick mass of cat-tails cut off and stuck in the mud around you in a marsh, or built by covering a frame with canvas or burlap. The simple blinds you see here will increase your chances of seeing birds close up.

Visit an area for a few days before putting up your blind so you will know the best place for it and the best time of day to use it. Even when you are out of sight, wildlife may not appear right away. Patience is very important because wild animals do not give "command performances." Make the blind large enough to allow you to sit comfortably. In addition to your binoculars, field guide and possibly a journal for taking notes, bring along something quiet to pass the time, such as food, a book or a puzzle. Your time and effort will be rewarded when you get close to wildlife, see them in their own homes and find out some of the fascinating secrets of their lives.

A body blind

You don't need to build or grow a fancy blind to hide from the birds. Try dressing in camouflage colours—greens and browns—so that you blend in with the background. Wear a hat, a long-sleeved shirt and long pants. This get-up will not only camouflage you so that you don't frighten off nervous birds; it'll also protect you from insect bites while you watch the wildlife.

Umbrella blind

Rain or shine, you can use this collapsible blind just about anywhere.

You'll need: a hammer
a stake or hollow aluminum pole
an umbrella (not a bright colour)
60 cm (2 feet) of bendable wire
safety pins
canvas or burlap (preferably brown or green)
heavy stones
scissors

1. Hammer your stake or pole into the ground in the centre of your site.
2. Using wire, attach the handle of an umbrella to the pole.
3. Using safety pins, fasten the cloth to the umbrella so that it extends right down to the ground on all sides to create a tent-like enclosure.
4. Weigh down the edges of the material with heavy stones.
5. Cut viewing holes at your eye-level all around the blind so you can see out in all directions.

A living blind

Grow your own blind and hide from the birds while adding pretty flowers to your garden.

You'll need: 1.2 m (4 feet) of binder twine
4 poles, 1.5-1.8 m (5-6 feet) high
a shovel
runner bean or morning glory seeds
string
cedar or pine boughs (optional)

1. Use the binder twine to lash your poles together in a teepee style.
2. Dig up a narrow strip of earth around the base of your blind for planting.
3. Plant the morning glory or runner bean seeds around three sides of your blind and care for them according to the directions on the package.

4. When the vines grow, tie them to your frame with string so that they grow up the poles. Not only will you have pretty flowers on your blind, but hummingbirds and butterflies may also visit the blossoms, giving you a really close-up view.
5. If you live in an area where planting vines is not possible, tie cedar or pine boughs to the frame instead.

Say it with a song

American Woodcock

You may feel like singing when you're very happy, but would you break into song if you were angry, afraid or hungry? Birds use songs to express all of these emotions. The main purpose of a bird's song is, however, to claim a breeding territory and to attract a mate.

No trespassing
When a male bird is preparing to mate in the spring, he first stakes out his breeding territory. Then he defends the invisible borders of his territory from other birds of the same species. In most cases, the defender sings a song. An intruding male hears the energetic sounds of the landlord and knows that it means, "No Trespassing." Actual battles are rarely necessary. Within his territory, the male chooses several singing perches. These are usually the tops of trees, posts or even TV antennae—anywhere the bird can sing out and be heard.

Love songs
Now that he's got a territory, the male needs a mate. A male bird may attract a female with his brilliant plumage, with a song or a special song and dance. Or he may try all three. The male American Woodcock catches the eye of his mate with an exciting performance. Starting with a nasal *peent* call from the ground, he then whirs upward, wings whistling loudly, dances about in the air and then drops back to the ground to continue calling.

Sing for your supper
Some bird songs are related to food. For instance, nestlings tell their parents they're hungry by cheeping in a certain way. Adults may call out to tell their young or each other about a source of food. The response is usually a noisy gathering of birds rushing in for the feast.

Unsung songs

How can a bird sing without opening its mouth? A bird's song is defined as one sound or a series of sounds, more or less in a row, produced in a definite pattern. The tapping of woodpeckers, the drumming of a grouse and the whistling of a snipe's feathers all count as bird songs.

Look and listen

You can identify birds not only by looking at them, but also by listening to them. After a while you may even learn to recognize a bird by its call alone. Although each species usually has two or more distinct songs, with variations, their general patterns can be recognized with some practice.

The mockingbird gets its name because it "mocks" (imitates) other birds' calls during the day. But at night it sings its own beautiful melody, repeating one pattern of notes several times, then moving on to a new one. It's a beautiful sound to fall asleep by. You *couldn't* fall asleep to the call of a Trumpeter Swan, though. It sounds like an old car horn. No wonder it's called a "trumpeter."

Some people remember bird calls by making up human words to fit the sound. For instance, some people think the Barred Owl is saying, "Who cooks for you?" The Olive-sided Flycatcher, on the other hand, chants "Quick, three beers." You can make up your own words to help you associate a particular bird call with its owner. Many records and tapes of bird calls are available so you can practise your bird song identification.

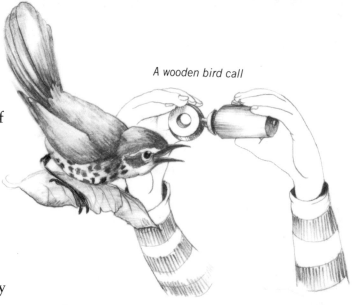

A wooden bird call

Some birdwatchers imitate a bird to coax it out of hiding. This is commonly done to get owls to fly into view, but will work in almost any bird's defended territory. Besides imitating a bird yourself, you can use various kinds of equipment to do it. Tape recordings of specific birds are often played to get a bird in the field to respond. There are also commercial bird callers, such as the Audubon Bird Call. It's a small, wooden noise box that you twist to make a bird-like sound.

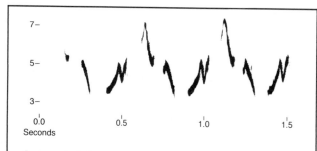

A sound picture
Scientists have developed a special way of writing down bird songs. Unlike the musical notes you are familiar with, a bird's song looks like this and is called an audiospectrogram or sonogram. It shows the pitch, volume (by line thickness) and tempo of the song.

Who cooks for you?

65

Pretty as a picture

Why not try combining two great hobbies: birdwatching and photography? That way you can record your birding triumphs on film and keep them as lasting memories. Although professionals use complex and expensive camera equipment, with practice you can get a lot of pleasure from a simple camera.

Candid camera

Many of your birdwatching skills can be applied to photography. For instance, being quiet and well hidden is very important not only so a bird will come close enough for a good picture, but also so that it will act naturally. You can hide yourself and your camera behind bushes or rocks. Or you can build a bird blind (see page 62). A blind is especially useful for photographing nesting birds without disturbing them. You can even stay in your house and take a photograph through an open window. If you are using a camera that gives you pictures instantly, your subject should be within a few feet for a really good picture. Experiment with some photos to get an idea of what distance is best.

Setting up

Backyards or local parks are good places to develop your skills. Choose an area with a nice background for a photo. For instance, berry-covered shrubs, a flower bed or an old stump will be much nicer than a clothesline, driveway or other non-natural feature. Once you have a location, try to attract birds to it by putting out bird seed or a bird bath. If you're using a blind, set it up so that you will have a good view of where the birds might land.

Picture this

One picture of a bird may show something about the bird's appearance or behaviour, but a series of pictures can tell a whole story. If you are watching a nest over a period of several days or weeks, take pictures often. When laid out in sequence, your pictures will show the bird's story from egg to fledgling.

You can also concentrate on one species of bird, say a robin. Photograph robins as they do different things such as perching, walking, flying, poking for worms, eating fruit or bathing. Put your pictures together in a story-like format to show others what a robin's life is like.

Lighten up

Lighting is an important part of your picture. When using a simple camera, make sure your subject is well lit, but do not point your camera into the sun when photographing. Try to ensure some contrast in your picture. For example, a dark-coloured bird will show up much better against a light-coloured background such as snow or sky than against a dark tree trunk or forest floor.

67

Sketching birds

You can take birdwatching one step further by sketching the birds you see. Because birds in the wild tend to move around a lot, or are well hidden, they can be difficult for a beginner to sketch. When starting out, use photographs or magazine pictures of birds or visit a museum and sketch the stuffed birds on display. Once you master the basic skills of sketching, you can move on to the birds outdoors.

You'll need: a soft pencil—B, 2B, 3B (No. 2) or softer
a pad of blank paper
a hard surface, such as a clipboard, to work on
photographs or pictures from bird magazines (optional)

Shaping up

Look at the basic outline of the bird illustrated here. Do any of the body parts remind you of basic shapes? All birds have oval bodies. It is what's attached to the bodies—the head, neck, feet, tail and feathers—that make each bird look different. Start out by drawing the biggest, simplest shape—the body—first.

Sizing up

Before you start drawing the body parts, look at the size of the bird's head, feet, tail and so on in relation to its body. For example, the owl's head is large compared to its body, but the ostrich has a very tiny head. Compare the lengths of body parts, too. Notice how long the ostrich's neck is, while the owl doesn't seem to have any neck at all.

Each bird beak has its own size and shape. Compare the size of the beak to the rest of the head. Notice that the macaw's beak is as wide as its head. On the other hand, this blue tit's beak is only as big as its eye. Where does the beak join the oval of the head? Is it pointing straight out or down? Check these details before adding the beak to your drawing.

Lining up

Here's a helpful hint to line up, or position, different parts of a bird's body in your sketch. Hold your pencil upright at arm's length in front of the bird. Close one eye and look up and down the pencil. Note the location of each body part with respect to this imaginary line formed by your pencil. The robin drawn here has its head and feet stretched over to the left of the pencil, while its wings and tail fall to the right. Try holding your pencil out horizontally, too. Note how this bird's head lines up with its outstretched wing.

Finishing up

Bring your bird to life by adding some details. Notice the direction from which the light is coming and shade in the shadows. Finally, add tones for the dark patches and special markings of your bird.

Birds and You

Making bird baths and gourmet bird food will make you the most popular bird lover in your neighbourhood. So roll up your sleeves and get to work!

Feed the birds

How can you get birds to visit your yard? Invite them for a meal! Feeding birds is not only fun; it's a great way to see birds up close and find out about their behaviour.

In areas where the winters are cold, many birds become dependent on feeders to help them get through the season. The energy they get from food helps keep them warm. Food supply, not temperature, is often the key to winter survival. Because of this, it is important to keep feeding your feathered friends once you start. Feed them all through the winter and into the spring, until nature can once again take over with its own supply of seeds, berries and insects.

Although you can go to a store and buy a ready-made birdfeeder, you can also make a terrific feeder out of a few easy-to-find materials. Try some of these ideas for attracting and feeding birds. Make several feeders and hang them around your garden or school yard.

Coconut feeder

You may think coconuts are for monkeys, but this one is for the birds!

You'll need: one coconut
a hand drill
a small saw
1-1.5 m (3-5 feet) of thin, bendable wire

1. Drill a hole in the coconut and drain out the milk.
2. Cut a quarter off one end of the coconut, using the saw. Ask an adult to help you do this so you don't cut yourself.

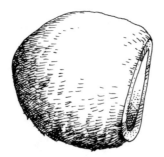

3. Drill two holes near the cut edge, one on either side. Thread the wire through the holes so that the coconut can be hung from a branch or other support as shown.

4. Some birds will eat the coconut meat, but you can also fill the cavity with seed as an added treat.

Things to watch for

Watch the birds that flock to your homemade feeder. You can discover a lot about them just by being a keen observer. Here are a few things to watch for:

▫ What kinds of food do different birds prefer? Birds, like people, have likes and dislikes when it comes to eating. You may find that woodpeckers, nuthatches and other insect-eaters are attracted by suet, while seed-eaters, such as Blue Jays and Evening Grosbeaks, prefer sunflower seeds.

▫ Where do the birds like to eat? Some birds, such as Blue Jays and cardinals, are happy feeding as high as 1.5 m (1.5 yards) or more above ground. Juncos, on the other hand, often eat on the ground, eating the seed spilled from feeders above.

▫ Which birds spend the longest time feeding? Different birds have very different eating habits. Chickadees, for instance, rush in for a quick nibble and rush away again, only to return within a minute or two to repeat the performance. On the other hand a Mourning Dove may gracefully glide in for a landing and settle down to eat at its leisure.

▫ Are some birds more aggressive than others? After you watch your feeder for a while, the "personalities" of birds begin to show. In general, small birds are scared off by larger and noisier ones. Aggressive species, such as starlings and Blue Jays, stand out in a crowd.

▫ What time of day is most popular for feeding? You may get a flurry of activity at your feeder at certain times of day. Once you have figured out the local feeding schedule, you can choose the best times for feeder watching.

Suet log feeder

Make a woodpecker's life easier with this simple-to-make feeder.

You'll need: a small log (about as long as your arm and a bit thicker) of poplar or birch
a hand drill
an eye-screw
30 cm (1 foot) of strong, bendable wire
suet

1. Make suet by melting beef fat (not pork because it's too salty) and then cooling it.
2. Drill several holes 1-2 cm (½ to ¾ of an inch) deep and 2.5 cm (1 inch) wide around your log. To get holes this big, use the largest drill bit and then enlarge the hole around the edges.
3. Attach an eye-screw to one end.
4. Fill the holes with suet.
5. Hang the log with wire from a branch.

Onion bag feeder

You can feed the birds and recycle at the same time. Use the net bag that onions come in to make this odour-free feeder.

You'll need: suet
net bag, like the ones onions are sold in (do not use wire mesh)
30 cm (1 foot) of string
birdseed

1. Make suet by melting beef fat (not pork because it's too salty) and then cooling it.
2. Shape the suet into a ball the size of a tennis ball and roll it in birdseed.
3. Place the ball in the net bag and hang it from a branch with string.

Pine cone feeder

Give nuthatches, chickadees and other insect-eaters a suet-stuffed treat.

You'll need: suet
peanut butter (optional)
pine cones (the short, squat cones of red pine work well)
an eye-screw
30 cm (1 foot) of string or thin, bendable wire

1. Make your suet by melting beef fat (not pork because it is too salty) and then cooling it.
2. Roll your pine cone in the suet or a mixture of suet and peanut butter so that the nooks and crannies are filled.

3. Insert an eye-screw in the cone as shown.
4. Attach a string or wire to the eye-screw and hang your feeder from a branch.

Peanut feeder

Here's a nutty idea for attracting birds to your garden or school yard. You may even get some squirrels, too.

You'll need: raw peanuts in the shell
string or yarn

1. Tie the peanuts in a row with your string or yarn.
2. Hang the string from a branch.

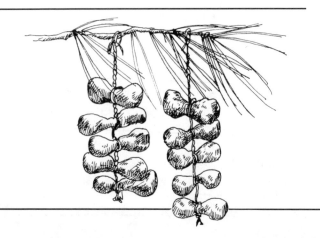

Tin can feeder

What do you get when you cross a juice can with two pie plates? A nifty birdfeeder of course!

You'll need: a clean tin can, such as a large juice can, with both ends removed
tin snips
2 foil pie plates
scissors
75 cm (2.5 feet) of strong, bendable wire
birdseed
60 cm (2 feet) of string

1. Ask an adult to cut two semi-circles on opposite sides of the bottom edge of your tin can with tin snips.

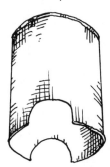

2. In each of your pie plates, make two small holes about 4 cm (1.5 inches) apart, near the middle.

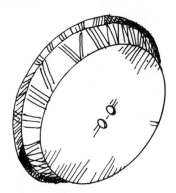

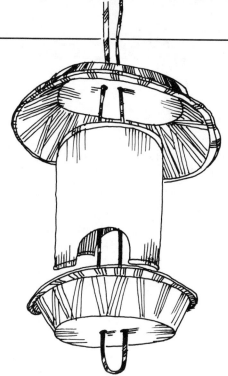

3. Assemble your materials as shown. Thread the wire through the pie plates and can so that the two loose ends are at the top.
4. Twist the ends of the wire together about 10 cm (4 inches) above the top pie plate.

5. Slide the top pie plate up the wire so that you can fill the can with seed. As the birds eat from the bottom tray, the seed will come through the semi-circles and refill the tray.
6. This feeder can be hung from a branch with string or placed on a table or other sturdy platform. Squirrels may help themselves at a table, though.
7. To refill the can, simply slide the top pie plate up the wires and pour in the seed.

Gardening for birds

Learning to be a good host or hostess to birds can be very rewarding and fun. If you give birds their four basic needs for survival, they will be only too happy to spend time in your yard. You must provide **food, water, shelter** where birds can hide from predators and bad weather and a safe and suitable **nesting area**. Backyard habitats can range from several hectares or acres right down to a verandah or window box. Here are some tips to get you started.

Size it up

As you're choosing plants to put into your garden, keep in mind that different birds prefer different sizes of flowers, bushes and trees.

- Red-eyed Vireos, tanagers and orioles prefer tall trees.
- Thrashers and cardinals nest in shrubs of medium height.
- Song Sparrows and Rufous-sided Towhees like low-growing plants.

In addition to varying heights, you will attract more species if you provide both dense cover and open area.

Gourmet gardening

Food is a main attraction for birds. By serving a smorgasbord of different foods, birds can pick and choose the food that they require.

- Robins and Cedar Waxwings will be delighted with a feast of berries.
- Cone feeders such as crossbills are attracted to conifers like pine and hemlock or alders and birch trees.
- Blue Jays, woodpeckers and even squirrels can be lured with the promise of a good acorn harvest from an oak tree.

Planting trees and shrubs is an excellent way to provide a variety of food and habitat for birds, but it takes good planning and lots of work and it can be expensive. Most of all it takes time. Many trees must grow for at least five years to provide suitable shelter and food. Shrubs are usually much faster growing and may be occupied within a year.

Flower power

For a faster, easier and cheaper source of food and cover, try flowers. They offer a rainbow of colour to beautify your garden and also provide seeds or nectar to satisfy hungry birds. Choose flowers that are suited to your local climate. Also choose flowers that will flourish in your garden's mini-climate: some flowers like shady areas, others prefer sunshine. The necessary information is usually on the back of seed packages.

Planting annuals (plants that die at the end of the growing season) is a good way to attract birds. Annuals produce large quantities of seeds, which serve as food for such birds as American Goldfinches and Dark-eyed Juncos. Popular annuals include sunflowers, zinnias, cosmos and asters.

Where to plant

When you hear someone say, "Tallest at the back and smallest at the front," you probably think of a group photo. But flowers can be planted the same way. Very tall varieties of sunflowers and zinnias, for example, look best at the back of a flower bed and provide a background for lower blooms. Some tall plants may need support. They can be propped up against fences or tied to stakes. Climbing plants, such as morning glories, will need support too. They do well near a wall they can climb. Whatever and wherever you're planting, think clumps. Plant a large clump of similar flowers together. This gives birds a large food supply in a small area. And always plant near shelter. Birds won't visit wide-open spaces far from a safe shelter.

Mini-gardens

Even if you have very limited space, or no yard at all, you can create a mini-garden with flower pots or a window box. Plant some attractive flowers with foliage in a window box, add a small dish of water and a container of birdseed and—presto!—you have a tiny habitat for birds. Or group together an assortment of flower pots containing different sizes and colours of annuals on front steps or wherever there is room.

Gourmet bird food

You don't have to be a great chef to whip up something tasty for your feathered friends. Try this simple recipe and make a delicious seed salad for the birds. You'll find the seeds you need for it in a health food store or plant nursery.

Super seed salad

You'll need: 250 mL (1 cup) cracked corn
250 mL (1 cup) millet (white proso is popular)
250 mL (1 cup) sunflower seeds in shell (black-striped or oil)
100 mL (½ cup) buckwheat
100 mL (½ cup) shelled peanuts
50 mL (¼ cup) coarse white sand or fine gravel (see Stone salad below)

1. Mix the ingredients together.
2. Store in a dry place.

Wild salad

If you're planning a trip in the country in the fall, collect lamb's quarter, dock, smartweed and ragweed seeds in open fields and along roadsides. Shake the seeds into a paper bag and mix them into your Super Seed Salad when you get home. The birds will go wild over your wild salad.

Stone salad
Sand or fine gravel are important ingredients in your bird salad. Why? It helps birds grind up their food. Birds don't have teeth to crush and grind up their food so that they can digest it. Instead they swallow food whole and grind it up in a thick-walled, muscular part of the stomach called the gizzard. Small stones and sand in the gizzard help with the grinding. They are called "gizzard stones."

Feed a hummingbird
The dazzling acrobatic displays of hummingbirds are a treat to watch, so it's worth the effort to attract them to your garden. Fortunately, hummingbirds are suckers for nectar. They actually stick their long bills into flowers and suck up the sweet nectar inside. They prefer red, orange or purple flowers with tube- or bell-shaped blossoms. Morning glories, lilies, petunias, hollyhocks, trumpet creepers, bonfire and fuchsia are all hummingbird tempters. When planting flowers rich in nectar, you may get an added bonus: butterflies.

Hanging baskets of fuchsia, red impatiens or similar flowers are irresistible to hummingbirds. They will visit these "hanging gardens" even when people are nearby.

Natural birdfeeders
Instead of cleaning up the garden after the plants die, leave the flower stalks standing. They will serve as natural birdfeeders for the birds over the winter.

Follow the food

What happens to the seeds and nuts eaten by birds? You can track the food from beginning to end by following the numbers in this see-through Blue Jay.

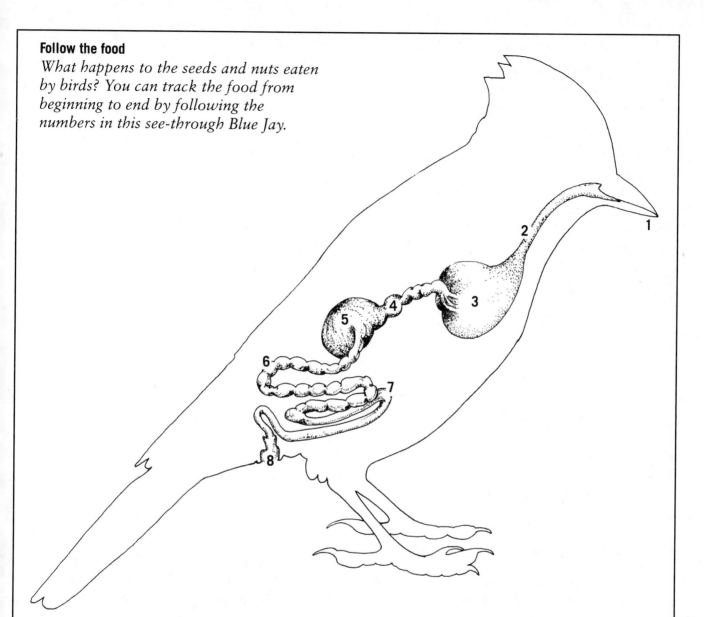

The seeds enter the bird's mouth (1) and travel down the esophagus (2) to the crop (3). The crop lets a bird pig out and store the food until later. Vultures, for instance, may eat so much at one sitting that their crop is overflowing. They may be too heavy to fly! The stored food can be digested when the bird is resting or sleeping, or it may be regurgitated and fed to baby birds.

From the crop, the food enters the stomach (4) and gizzard (5), where it is ground up. The food wastes that are not digested travel out of the bird by way of the small (6) and large intestines (7) and the cloaca (8). Some people call the result bird poop, but its technical name is guano.

79

Making a bird bath

With a few household materials you can make a great bird bath to keep your feathered friends clean and happy. Even in winter, birds still bathe and drink, so your bird bath can be a year-round meeting place. If the water in your bird bath freezes in winter, you'll need to rig up a heater. ASK AN ADULT TO HELP YOU BECAUSE THIS CAN BE DANGEROUS. Place a small aquarium heater in the bird bath and plug it in with a heavy-duty, outdoor extension cord. What happens when there is no unfrozen water to drink? Luckily, birds can quench their thirst by picking at snow and ice.

Bird bath tips
Your bird bath should have:
- a non-slippery surface (by thinly coating a surface with white glue and sprinkling sand over it, you will have a good surface)
- gently sloping sides
- a maximum depth of 8 cm (3 inches)
- some shade
- nearby dense vegetation for cover

Clean the bath often and keep it filled with water.

A hanging or sunken bird bath

This bird bath comes in two versions—a hanging bath and an in-ground model. Whichever you choose, your bird bath will be a hit with the locals.

You'll need: 2 pieces of binder twine, each about 1.2 m (4 feet) long
a large pottery plant saucer or large earthenware pie plate

1. Place your two pieces of twine on the floor to form an X. Make a knot where the twine meets.
2. Place your saucer on the twine so that the knot is beneath the centre of the saucer.

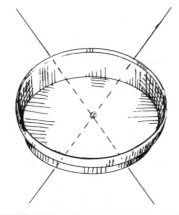

3. Carefully gather the four ends of the twine above the saucer and tie a double knot.
4. Hang your saucer from a branch and fill it with water.

5. To make a sunken bird bath, place the saucer in a hole in the ground so that the edges are level with the ground. WARNING: if there are neighbourhood cats around, use the hanging bird bath instead of the sunken version.

Wetcleaning, drycleaning and ants

Most birds, unlike some kids, love having a bath. In wild areas, birds look for ponds, streams and springs for bathing and drinking. Even birds passing overhead may make a pit stop if they hear the sound of running or dripping water. Most birds bathe to keep clean and to cool off during hot weather. Hummingbirds, however, take baths several times a day just for fun.

Many birds take two kinds of baths — a water bath to get clean and a dust bath to get rid of parasites, such as lice and mites. Some ornithologists (scientists who study birds)

believe that dust baths also help birds sandblast their feathers, cleaning them and restoring their insulation value.

Perhaps the strangest way some birds have of getting clean is by rubbing live ants into their feathers. Jays, robins, sparrows and other songbirds use their beaks to rub the ants in. Or they stand on an anthill and let the ants climb up onto their bodies. Sound like a scene from a science fiction movie? Some ornithologists think the ants produce certain chemicals that kill bird parasites.

An added attraction

Birds are enchanted by the sound of running or dripping water, so why not let them have it!

You'll need: a nail
a plastic bucket
a small piece of cotton material
60 cm (2 feet) of binder twine

1. Use the nail to poke a hole in the bottom of your bucket.
2. Stick the piece of cotton through the hole so that it hangs down.
3. Use the twine to hang your bucket in a tree directly over your bird bath.
4. Fill the bucket with water daily. The piece of cotton will soak up water and cause it to drip down into the bird bath.

A dust bath

Sometimes birds like to give themselves a thorough "drycleaning" with dust. Here's how to make a dust bath.

You'll need: a shallow box
5-8 cm (2-3 inches) of roadside dust

1. Place the dust in the box.
2. Put the box in a sheltered area outside.
3. Refill the box as necessary.

Operation rescue

If you find a young bird alone in the grass, what do you do? In most cases, the answer should be, "Nothing." Although the bird may look abandoned, its parents may be watching it from a nearby bush, gathering food or looking after other young. Hawk, owl, woodpecker and songbird chicks leave the nest before they can fly or take care of themselves. They are called altricial birds. The parents still look after them, but are not always visible. Other birds, such as ducks, geese, plovers and grouse, can look for food when they are only a few hours old. They are called precocial birds. Although out alone, they are still largely defenceless and their parents continue to care for them. So, if you find a bird and suspect it is an orphan, watch it carefully for an hour or so to be sure the parents aren't nearby. Only then should you think about caring for it yourself.

Giving a lift

Strong winds may blow a nestling or nest out of a tree. The nest should be put back in the tree as high as you can reach. A nestling should be returned to its nest, if possible. If the baby bird seems cold, cup your hands around it to warm it up. Once the bird is back in bed, place a hand over the nest to make it appear dark. This will help calm the bird and encourage it to snuggle down into the nest. Parents will not abandon their young just because you have touched them. Adult birds may, however, abandon a nest if it is disturbed during construction or soon after the eggs are laid.

A helping hand

If you do find an orphaned bird, take it indoors and give it shelter, warmth and food. A young altricial bird is like a human baby; it needs almost constant attention and eats a great deal. The best thing for the bird is for you to contact an animal care expert as soon as possible. In the meantime, here are some tips for keeping your guest happy and healthy.

A new nest

Make a cosy nest for the bird in a berry box or similar small container. Use shredded paper towels or tissues for a soft lining. Mother birds keep their babies warm by cuddling them close to their bodies. You will have to be the mother in this case and provide heat for the young bird. Put the new nest on a heating pad set on low or hang a light bulb over the nest. Very young birds with few or no feathers need a temperature of about 35° C (95° F). Down-covered nestlings should be kept at about 27° C (80° F).

Fast food

Very young birds should be fed every 15 minutes during daylight hours; otherwise, they'll slowly starve. But birds with feathers may only need to eat once an hour. Do not give water to young birds. What do you feed a baby bird? Try the recipes in the box on this page.

If you are caring for an adult bird, try to identify it. Use a good bird book to find out what it normally eats. Pet stores sell meal worms for insect eaters and seed mixtures for seed eaters. If you are not sure what to provide, give a bit of everything and let the bird decide. Leave the food out so the adult bird can feed on its own and provide a shallow dish of water for drinking and bathing.

Baby bird formula

This recipe is for helpless (altricial) baby birds, such as owls, hawks and songbirds.

You'll need: 25 mL (2 tbsp) water
25 mL (2 tbsp) milk
2 egg yolks
Pablum
vitamin drops

1. Mix the water, milk and egg yolks together in the top of a double boiler. Put water in the bottom of the double boiler and cook for 10 minutes over medium heat.
2. Add Pablum, a little at a time, until mixture is thick.
3. Add two or three vitamin drops and stir.
4. Use a large-holed medicine dropper for feeding.

Baby food for ducks and geese

Since the babies of some birds, such as ducks, geese, plovers and grouse, can eat by themselves, your job is easier.

You'll need: 3 hard-boiled egg yolks

1. Finely chop the yolks and spread them on a rough surface, such as wood.
2. Let the young bird scratch and feed as long as it wants.

Letting go

Try to get an animal care expert to look after any wildlife you find in trouble. If you must adopt it temporarily, don't forget that your orphan is a wild creature, not a pet. Young birds should be released back into their natural habitat as soon as their tail feathers grow in. Adults can be freed when they are able to look after themselves. In many areas there are laws against keeping wild birds. You may even need a permit to nurse an injured bird back to health. Call a local wildlife officer or conservation officer for information.

Birds beware

You've probably watched cartoons about Wile E. Coyote and the Roadrunner. That poor coyote gets run over by trains, blasted with dynamite and regularly falls off the edge of cliffs. But nothing ever happens to the bird. Real life is much more hazardous to birds. Egg-lovers sometimes rob their nests, cats pounce on them and bad weather can cause them to freeze or starve. But the biggest hazard is living near people.

S.O.S.
Many lighthouses in North America have a revolving light at night to help ships navigate. Birds are attracted to the light, especially during stormy weather. Many birds die after crashing into the lighthouse or nearby obstacles such as guy wires. In Europe, some lighthouses have changed their lights from white to blue. Instead of using a revolving light, they now use a flashing light that gives a one-second flash every ten seconds. Because the light is not constant, birds don't seem to be drawn to it as much and fewer die.

Shocking
Larger birds, such as herons, waterfowl and birds of prey, sometimes run into telephone wires and power lines. Some species perch on top of hydro poles and can be electrocuted. The easiest way to solve this problem is for telephone and power companies to place the wires in areas where few birds travel.

Dangerous diving

Seabirds diving for fish face a different problem. Instead of running into tall objects, they collide with objects under water. Many diving ducks, loons, murres and Dovekies drown when they get caught in the huge fish nets set by fishermen or the lost and castaway nets that clutter the oceans.

Things that go bump in the night

Birds fly into the mirror-like windows of office buildings daily, but it is the night-time collisions that are the biggest problem. Many birds migrate in huge numbers at night. When weather is poor, they may fly low or have to land and find shelter. This is when the highest number of deaths occur. Because most office buildings are lit up at night, birds are attracted to them. They will fly directly to the light, hitting the building or the light itself. Injured birds sometimes fall to the ground and become trapped in the courtyards of buildings and cannot escape. Most of the injured or dead birds are vireos and warblers.

All of these dangers to birds are caused by people. While some of the hazards are now being reduced, experts are hard at work to find new ways of protecting more birds. You can help by bird-proofing the outside of your windows at your home, apartment or school. Turn the page to find out how.

Bird-proofing your windows

Have you ever accidentally walked into sliding glass doors without seeing them? Large, clean windows are beautiful to look through but they can be dangerous, especially for birds. Why would a bird hit your window?

- The reflection of flowers and shrubs in the window confuses the bird. Believing another garden lies ahead, the bird flies into the window.
- A male bird may see its own reflection and think there is a competing male invading its territory. It then flies at the window to attack the intruder.
- Sometimes windows are arranged in a house so that there appears to be a passage right through the house. A bird in the backyard may think it can fly right through to the front yard . . . until it hits the window.

Hang-ups

Help prevent the injury and death of birds, especially during migration, by trying one or all of these ideas.

1. Hang tinkling or glittering objects in problem windows. Try strips of tin foil or wind chimes.
2. Reduce reflection by tacking up some light, see-through screening over the glass.
3. Make a hawk to put up in your window. Visiting songbirds will think it is a real predator and be very careful to avoid the window.

You'll need: a sheet of thin white paper for tracing
glue
light cardboard, from a cereal box or gift box
scissors
black magic-marker or crayon
30 cm (1 foot) of string
tape
thumb tack

1. Trace this hawk onto a piece of paper.
2. Glue the paper onto some light cardboard.
3. Cut the cardboard to the shape of the hawk.
4. Colour your hawk dark black on both sides.
5. Tape a string to the hawk's head and attach the other end of the string to the outside of your window frame using a thumb tack. Your hawk will work best if it can move freely in the wind.

First aid

If you find a bird that has become stunned or hurt after hitting a window, take it indoors and place it in a medium-sized covered box. After a few hours' rest it will probably be recovered and you can let it go. For more serious injuries see **Operation Rescue** *on pages 82–83.*

Going, going, gone?

What do Whooping Cranes, Peregrine Falcons and Kirtland's Warblers have in common? They are all endangered bird species. When a bird is called endangered, it's a warning to everyone that the species needs help right now. Whatever problem has caused the population to drop so drastically, it must be solved immediately. If something isn't done, the species will probably become extinct. Extinction means that no more individuals of a species are alive anywhere in the world—they are gone forever. The Passenger Pigeon, Great Auk, Carolina Parakeet and Labrador Duck are examples of extinct North American birds.

Snowy Egret

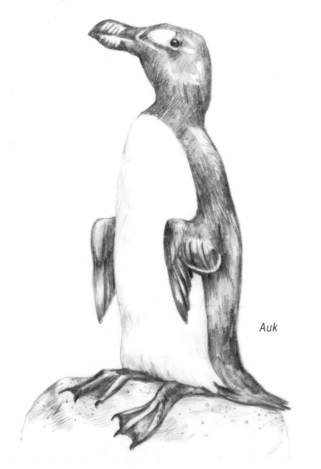

Auk

Why are they going?

If someone took away your home and food and you couldn't find anywhere else to go, your life would be in danger. That's what is happening to animals all over the world. Their habitat is being destroyed and they have nowhere else to live, feed, breed or hide from enemies. For example, when a marsh is drained, hundreds of species may lose their homes. Habitat loss is the biggest problem facing endangered species.

In the past, some species became endangered or extinct because of over-hunting. People robbed nests for eggs and killed birds in huge numbers for food and feathers. Passenger Pigeons, Trumpeter Swans and some herons and egrets all suffered because people wanted their beautiful feathers for fashionable hats and clothing.

Pollution is another hazard facing wildlife. Pesticides such as DDT have poisoned many birds of prey.

Whoop, whoop, hurray!

Fortunately, there are many projects to help endangered species around the world. Conservation groups, governments and private companies are joining together to help save a variety of species. The Whooping Crane is a terrific example of how two countries—Canada and the United States—have worked together to help wildlife. The Whooping Crane spends its winters in Aransas, Texas, and breeds during the summer in northern Alberta. With the help of laws, research, public education and careful habitat protection, the Whooping Crane population has risen from a low of 21 in 1941 to an estimated 134 in 1987.

Individuals can help, too. For example, George Archibald, founder of the International Crane Association, helped a female Whooping Crane named Tex lay her eggs. Tex wasn't laying any eggs, and Dr. Archibald thought he knew why. She had lived near humans all her life and wasn't attracted to other birds. In order to lay an egg, Tex first had to do a mating dance. So Dr. Archibald filled in as her partner. For five mating seasons he and Tex danced. Finally in 1981 Tex mated with another Whooper and had a baby named Gee Whiz. Dr. Archibald said he felt like a father.

Whooping Crane

You can do it

The problems may seem huge, but you can do your part to save endangered species. How?

- Spread the word. The more people know about a problem, the more they'll care and want to help.
- Support a group that is helping endangered species. You can give them money or volunteer your time. By staging fundraising activities such as bake sales, car washes and raffles, children all over the world are raising money for research and protection for wildlife.
- Write letters to governments about what you think should be done to help wildlife.
- Learn more about endangered wildlife yourself. Visit libraries and write to government wildlife offices and conservation groups for up-to-date information.
- Get involved in a community conservation project. Local groups can do very important work, from building and setting out bluebird houses to putting up signs to protect endangered Piping Plover nesting areas.

Bothersome birds

Have you got competition for the cherries, strawberries or peaches in your garden? It's not surprising that some birds also like to harvest your crops; summer fruits taste good to them, too. How can you discourage birds from freeloading in your fruit and vegetable gardens without driving them away from the rest of your yard? A few harmless, homemade creations should do the trick.

Scarecrow

This "bird discourager" is fun to make and adds character to your garden. Traditionally scarecrows have been stuffed with straw, but you can also use cotton rags or even scrunched-up plastic bags.

You'll need: an old broom
a coat hanger (wood or plastic)
heavy tape
an old, plain pillow case
string and scissors
magic markers
old clothes (long-sleeved shirt, jeans, hat and gloves)
lots of straw, old rags or plastic bags for stuffing
elastic bands

1. Attach a coat hanger to the broom as shown. Fasten it on securely with heavy tape.

2. Put a pillow case over the straw part of the broom. Stuff this head with straw, old rags or bunched-up plastic bags. Tie it shut with string.

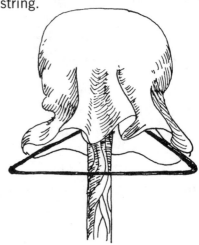

3. Draw on a face with magic markers and put on a hat.

4. Dress your scarecrow in old clothes. Use safety pins to attach the pants to the shirt. Stuff the clothes and tie the openings closed.

5. Choose a good spot in the garden for your scarecrow. ''Plant'' the broom handle into the ground.

6. For added effect, tie foil plates or tinsel to the hat or arms to help discourage birds. A fake owl sitting on the scarecrow's shoulder might also keep the birds from raiding your garden.

Tinfoil trees

Many birds are frightened by shining objects that move around or make noise. You can help to protect your fruit trees by hanging several foil pie plates from the branches, using string. The easier they swing in the breeze, the better. You might also try putting wind chimes in the tree to discourage the birds.

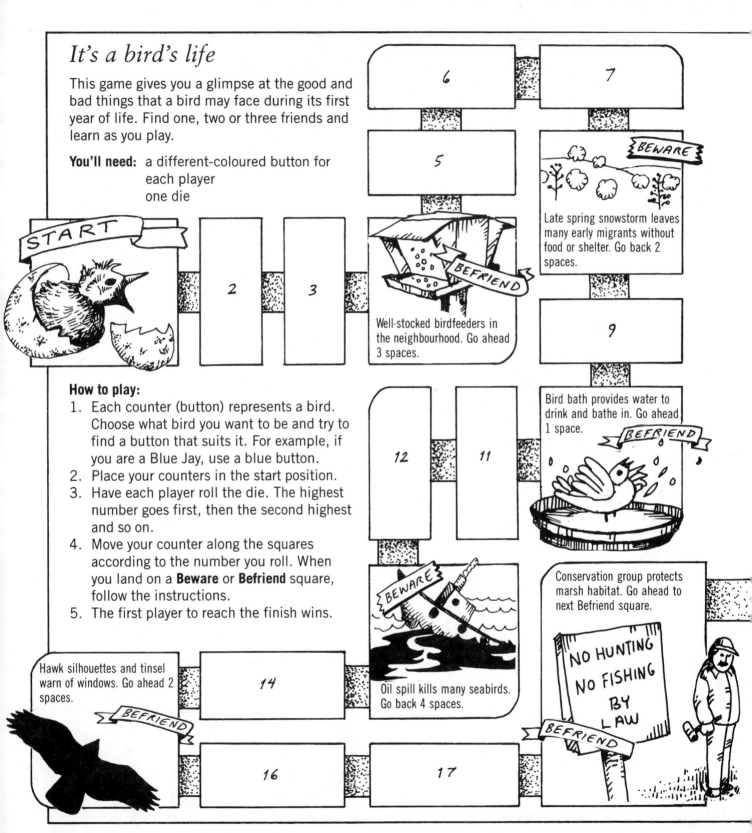

It's a bird's life

This game gives you a glimpse at the good and bad things that a bird may face during its first year of life. Find one, two or three friends and learn as you play.

You'll need: a different-coloured button for each player
one die

START

2   3

5

6   7

BEWARE

Late spring snowstorm leaves many early migrants without food or shelter. Go back 2 spaces.

BEFRIEND

Well-stocked birdfeeders in the neighbourhood. Go ahead 3 spaces.

9

Bird bath provides water to drink and bathe in. Go ahead 1 space.

BEFRIEND

How to play:

1. Each counter (button) represents a bird. Choose what bird you want to be and try to find a button that suits it. For example, if you are a Blue Jay, use a blue button.
2. Place your counters in the start position.
3. Have each player roll the die. The highest number goes first, then the second highest and so on.
4. Move your counter along the squares according to the number you roll. When you land on a **Beware** or **Befriend** square, follow the instructions.
5. The first player to reach the finish wins.

12   11

BEWARE

Oil spill kills many seabirds. Go back 4 spaces.

Conservation group protects marsh habitat. Go ahead to next Befriend square.

NO HUNTING
NO FISHING
BY
LAW

BEFRIEND

Hawk silhouettes and tinsel warn of windows. Go ahead 2 spaces.

BEFRIEND

14

16   17

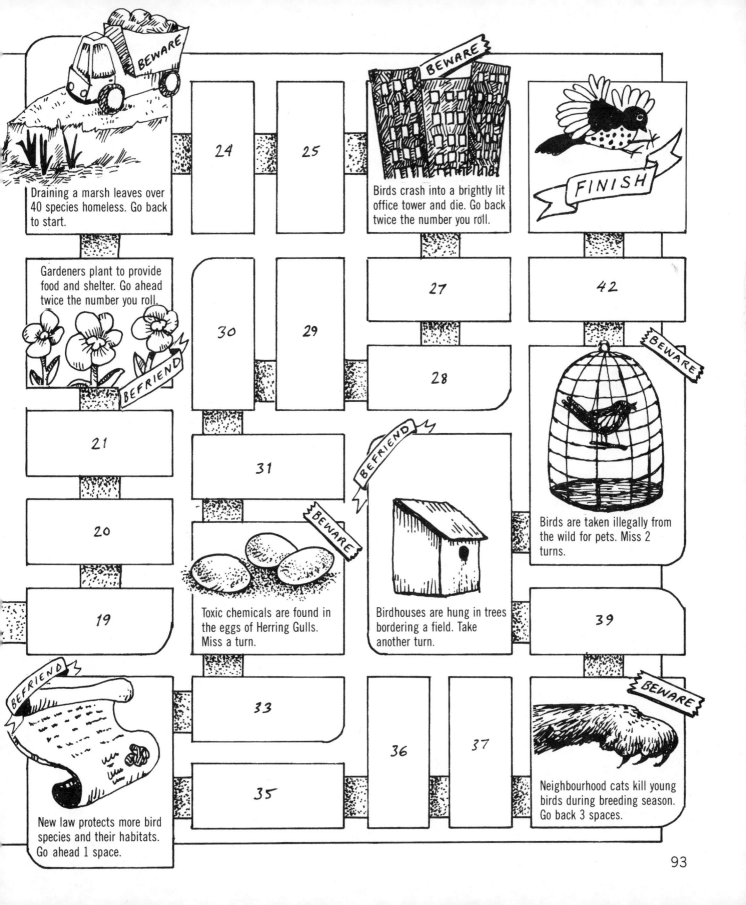

Draining a marsh leaves over 40 species homeless. Go back to start.

24

25

Birds crash into a brightly lit office tower and die. Go back twice the number you roll.

FINISH

Gardeners plant to provide food and shelter. Go ahead twice the number you roll.

BEFRIEND

30

29

27

42

28

21

31

BEFRIEND

Birds are taken illegally from the wild for pets. Miss 2 turns.

20

BEWARE

19

Toxic chemicals are found in the eggs of Herring Gulls. Miss a turn.

Birdhouses are hung in trees bordering a field. Take another turn.

39

BEFRIEND

33

36

37

BEWARE

New law protects more bird species and their habitats. Go ahead 1 space.

35

Neighbourhood cats kill young birds during breeding season. Go back 3 spaces.

93

INDEX

Answers

Bird Parts, Page 6
An owl plunged to the ground and attacked a mouse.

Take a peek at a beak, page 10
The pelican eats fish; the hummingbird eats nectar; the swift eats insects; the cardinal eats seeds; the waxwing eats berries; the hawk eats mice (and other small mammals).

Can you spot the foster baby?, page 30
The baby about to eat is the foster baby. It's a cowbird.

Some Birds Up Close, page 42
Here's who's who:

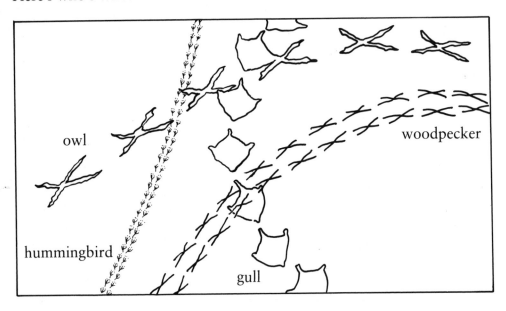